The

GREAT
GOLF COURSES
OF AMERICA

The

GREAT GOLF COURSES OF AMERICA

by John Gordon

Photography by Michael French

FIREFLY BOOKS

A Firefly Book

Front Cover photograph: Kapalua Golf Club (Plantation Course)

Design: Diane Farenick, Mercer Digital Design
Digital Golf Maps: Diane Farenick and Kimberley Young
Editorial Services: Harry Endrulat
Production Manager: Nick Pitt

Cataloguing in Publication Data

Gordon, John (John William)
    The great golf courses of America

ISBN 1-55209-149-X

1. Golf courses - United Sates. 1. Title

GV975.G672 1997   796.352'06'873   C97-931248-5

Published in the United States by
Firefly Books (U.S.) Inc.
P.O. Box 1338, Ellicott Station
Buffalo, NY 14205

Published in Canada by
Firefly Books Ltd.
3680 Victoria Park Ave.
Willowdale, Ont. M2H 3K1

Produced by Warwick Publishing Inc.

Printed in Canada

To the world's greatest family:
my incredibly understanding wife Leslie
and our fabulous children:
Will, Alexandra, and, especially,
Maggie, the best two-year-old
editorial assistant in history.

ACKNOWLEDGMENTS

Although my name is on it, literally scores of people have had a hand in compiling this book. First among them is Michael French (well, his name is on it too) who is responsible for the spectacular photography. Jim Williamson, Nick Pitt, Harry Endrulat, and Diane Farenick were the people at Warwick Publishing who shepherded the project through some turbulent times. Thanks for your patience.

Of invaluable assistance were the personnel of most clubs and, in some cases, their advertising and public relations companies, including Kim Anderson (Troon); Joanne Carlson and Clay Daniels (Bay Hill); Carole Doremus (Sea Pines Company); Melody Dossenbach (Pinehurst); Jennifer Greene of Middleton & Gendron (Ventana Canyon); Scott Head (Princeville); Susan Hruska (Homestead); Reid Nelson (Wild Dunes); Valerie Ramsey and Molly Joest (Pebble Beach Company); Joe Root (Mauna Kea); and Greg Wolf (Muirfield Village).

Almost all of the clubs in *The Great Golf Courses of America* exhibited class and enthusiasm when contacted about the book. Staff and members of several clubs went above and beyond my expectations in their efforts, including Dave Bryan (Southern Hills), Peter Burford (Merion), Timothy Hayes (Scioto), Henry Nichols (Shinnecock Hills), Bob Philbrick and Diana Banning (Prairie Dunes), Roger Regimbal (Plainfield), Dennis Roberson (Colonial), Eric Rule (Oak Hill), Geoff Shackelford (Riviera), Douglas Smith (Winged Foot), and Robert Trebus (Baltusrol). Several of the aforementioned have authored the histories of their clubs, which made for some great reading. Thanks again. You are a credit to the game.

The choices for this book were cross-referenced from various lists and then discussed with other knowledgeable sources, such as some of my former colleagues in golf administration, including Ted Blofsky (Northern California GA), Rick Coe (Oklahoma GA), Dennis Davenport (Chicago District GA), Steve Foehl (New Jersey State GA), Ross Galarneault (Minnesota GA), Ed Gowan (Arizona GA), Dick Haskell (Massachusetts GA), Cal Korf (Florida State GA), Brett Marshall (GA of Michigan), Tom Morgan (Southern California GA), Jay Mottola (Metropolitan GA), Jack Nance (Carolinas GA), David Norman (Virginia State GA), Bill Penn (Texas GA), Jim Popa (Ohio GA), Kim Richey (Kansas GA), Warren Simmons (Colorado GA), Jim Sykes (GA of Philadelphia), and Mike Waldron (Georgia State GA). Thanks for taking time out of (what I know from first-hand experience is) a very busy schedule!

In addition to club histories and other sources, several books were of great help in providing perspective and background: *The Golf Course* and *The Architects of Golf* by Geoffrey Cornish and Ronald Whitten, *The Confidential Guide to Golf Courses* by Tom Doak, and *Golf Courses of the PGA Tour* by George Peper. I highly recommend them for any golfer. Thanks also to my friends Tony, Joe, and James at Golf Gap in Toronto — a great place for golf books, golf talk, and everything else golf. Bob Weeks, the associate publisher of *Score*, Canada's golf magazine, was there to bail me out on some details. To Buddha Mike, Odd-Or-Even Johnny, Four-Hour Eddy, Scratch-And-Win Brad, and the rest of the usual suspects who slash around with me at Midland G&CC, thanks for the laughs. Here's to many more.

Marc Rochette, one of the finest photographers on the continent, took time out from his own birthday party to take the author photo. Thanks, Marc, and I'll talk to those responsible to make sure your name is spelled right this time.

The final and most heartfelt acknowledgment goes to my friend, Jim Fitchette, the late, great "Rex Revere." He was everything good in golf and showed me how to love the game.

John Gordon

TABLE OF CONTENTS

INTRODUCTION

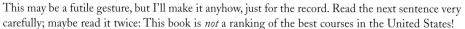

This may be a futile gesture, but I'll make it anyhow, just for the record. Read the next sentence very carefully; maybe read it twice: This book is *not* a ranking of the best courses in the United States!

Ranking courses, as such, seems to have become a necessary evil in the past dozen years or so. And I say that as a ranking panelist for two major magazines, one in Canada and one in the U.S. In fact, I started the ranking trend in Canada when I was managing editor of *Score* magazine, the national golf publication. Mea culpa. Granted, there are some positive aspects to this phenomenon; not the least of which is that it sells magazines and advertising. One recent publication even goes so far as to differentiate between modern and classical courses. (Give me a break.) But I digress.

This book is a cross section of some of the best layouts in America. You stroll through these pages and visit great courses from coast to coast, enjoying the spectrum of design, history, geography, topography, and so on. Some are private, some public, some resorts. Most of us will never have a chance to play Pine Valley, Seminole, or Augusta National, but isn't it great to dream? On the other hand, anyone can play Kapalua or Harbour Town. And who knows, a golfing acquaintance may have a friend who is a member at Shinnecock Hills or Winged Foot.

Selecting and writing about the courses was just part of the procedure. Photographer Michael French, who has teamed up with me on two previous golf books, spent weeks welded to the seat of his truck, hopscotching across the country to capture the essence of the final choices. He covered almost 20,000 miles, shooting more than 400 rolls of film in the process. (No, he didn't drive to Hawaii.) He packed only the essentials into his vehicle: cameras, lenses, golf clubs, mountain bike, and...cappuccino maker. That last item stood him in good stead when he was storm-stayed for two days in the mountains of North Carolina. In addition to fancy coffeemakers, our collaboration process also required 500 faxes, $10,000 in telephone calls, and mounds of books, scorecards, yardage guides, videos, and other resource materials.

Whether or not you agree with the courses we selected is immaterial. These choices are intended to delight the golfer's eye and ignite their imagination. We think we accomplished that goal. We hope you agree.

John Gordon

The par-3 12th hole at Augusta National represents the deceptively beautiful heart of Amen Corner, one of the most intimidating three-hole stretches in the game.

──────── *Augusta, Georgia* ────────

AUGUSTA

National Golf Club

Architects: Alister Mackenzie, Robert T. Jones Jr.
Opened for Play: 1933

Augusta National Golf Club is the legacy of the finest amateur golfer ever to walk the earth: Robert Tyre Jones Jr. More familiar to most golfers as "Bobby" Jones, he teamed with two other influential individuals — Alister Mackenzie and Clifford Roberts — without whom, it could be argued, the mystique of Augusta National would never have been created.

In 1930, at the tender age of 28, Jones had won all there was to win on both continents at a time when both the status and caliber of amateur golf stood head and shoulders above its professional counterpart. An enigmatic yet charismatic man, Jones decided to retire from competition and devote his time to business and the building of his "dream course," as he called his vision. Having visited Cypress Point on California's Monterey Peninsula and leaving impressed with how the

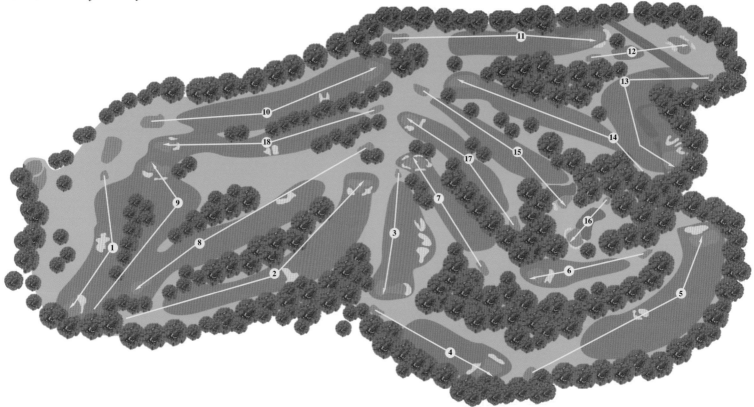

AUGUSTA NATIONAL GOLF CLUB
AUGUSTA, GEORGIA

HOLE	YARDAGE	PAR			
1	400	4	10	485	4
2	555	5	11	455	4
3	360	4	12	155	3
4	205	3	13	465	5
5	435	4	14	405	4
6	180	3	15	500	5
7	360	4	16	170	3
8	535	5	17	400	4
9	435	4	18	405	4
OUT	3,465	36	IN	3,440	36
			TOTAL	6,905	72

course architect, Mackenzie, had worked within the topography and natural features of the property, Jones knew all that remained was to find the right piece of land.

With the help of Roberts, a New York banker who vacationed in Augusta, Jones found 365 acres that had been developed as an arboretum and nursery for more than 70 years. As a result, the majestic stands of stately Georgia pines were now side by side on rolling hills with almost every known species of trees, flowers, and shrubs. "It seems that this land had been lying here for years just waiting for someone to lay a golf course on it," Jones wrote several years later. Although the fragrant and spectacular camellias and azaleas caught Jones's eye, it would be for the magnolias lining the driveway up to the manor house that Augusta National would become famous. The house remains today as the clubhouse, one of the most recognizable landmarks in golf. Roberts, Jones's partner, would become just as recognizable an Augusta landmark: He ramrodded the operations of both the golf club and the Masters until his death in 1977.

In Mackenzie, Jones found another kindred spirit. The two worked closely together, focusing on four guiding principles: "1. A really great course must be pleasurable to the

The gorgeous setting at the 13th green belies the difficulty of this final hole on the Amen Corner.

Mid-irons struck from the elevated tee of the par-3 sixth hole at Augusta National must stick close to the hole for any chance at birdie.

greatest possible number. 2. It must require strategy as well as skill or it cannot be enduringly interesting. 3. It must give the average player a fair chance and at the same time require the utmost from the expert who tries for subpar rounds. 4. All natural beauty should be preserved, natural hazards utilized, and a minimum of artificiality introduced." There can be no debate that these two geniuses fulfilled all four goals.

As Geoffrey Cornish and Ron Whitten comment in their outstanding book, *The Golf Course,* "Jones, who, like Mackenzie, was a devout admirer of St. Andrews, strongly felt alternative routes should be provided for players of lesser ability. But he also felt there should be rewards, especially on par-5 holes, for those who took a chance and succeeded. At Augusta, every hole looked deceptively simple; and, indeed, a high-handicap golfer could keep the ball in play for an enjoyable round. But every hole had a preferred target, a spot from which it was most advantageous to play the next stroke. Augusta National could yield low rounds, but only to a golfer who thought his way around the course."

The second hole at Augusta National is a 555-yard par 5 where Nick Faldo drained a 100-foot birdie putt in 1989 on his way to donning the green jacket, emblematic of a Masters victory.

How appropriate for a course inspired by Jones, the most cerebral of players.

Mackenzie and Jones did more than design a superb test of golf; they invented the spectator golf course. Greens were situated so as to be visible from nearby hillsides and, in some cases, mounds were built to provide additional vantage points. But now that Jones had his player's course, who would play it? As always, Jones had an answer, and in 1934, the first Masters (although it was then called simply the Annual Invitation Tournament) was held at Augusta. The venue and the event would become synonymous; in the minds of many golfers, "that course" in Georgia is called "The Masters." For 51 weeks of the year, the gates of the Augusta Club open only for the handful of members; but even they can't play the course itself from May to October when it is closed.

Although Mackenzie and Jones remain the architects of record — despite the fact that Jones referred to himself as a "consultant," hitting thousands of shots into proposed landing areas and greens — many more designers have touched this hallowed acreage: George Cobb, Perry Maxwell, Robert Trent Jones, Tom and George Fazio, Joseph Finger, Byron Nelson, Jay Morrish, Bob Cupp, Scott Miller, and even six-time Masters champion Jack Nicklaus. It is a credit to the integrity of the original design and the high esteem in which all these men hold Augusta National that the course remains one of the truest tests for all levels of golfers in the world.

In modern terms, Augusta National lacks many things that golfers take for granted in a

Amen Corner

The 12th hole at Augusta National has witnessed more heartbreak than just about any other hole in golf. The heart of Amen Corner, which starts on the 11th and concludes on the 13th, demands a high, precise short-iron which must land softly so as to avoid spinning back into Rae's Creek. Many players regard this deceptively striking par 3 as one of the hardest short holes in golf. No doubt primary among them is Tom Weiskopf, who once carded a 10-over-par 13 here. That total remains the highest score ever recorded on any hole in Masters history.

truly tough course. It is not overwhelmingly long, the rough is practically nonexistent, and the layout, in general, is straightforward. Instead, the resolute refusal of Augusta to surrender is based on more subtle challenges, primarily the treacherous, spine-chilling greens. The slopes and undulations range from almost unnoticeable to canyonlike; the speed of the putting surface cannot be overstated. All the analogies — the bottom of a bathtub, the hood of a car, and so on — only hint at the terrifying pace of these bent grass purgatories. In 1994, TV commentator Gary McCord said the greens were so fast, they must have been "bikini-waxed." Tournament organizers complained and McCord was not invited back to subsequent Masters.

But McCord's facetious observation should not be allowed to linger as a closing comment on Augusta National and its Masters. Rather, leave it to Ben Hogan: "Dignity is the keynote here, where the game of golf is elevated to the high position it deserves."

The back nine at Augusta National, the holes most familiar to TV viewers, begins with a long par 4 that wends its way through some of the stunning trees and flowering shrubs the course is famous for.

——————— *Springfield, New Jersey* ———————

BALTUSROL

Golf Club

Architect: A. W. Tillinghast
Opened for Play: 1895

The name of Baltusrol owes its origins to an unfortunate farmer, Baltus Roll, who had his brains beaten out by two rather inept thieves in 1831. His legacy lives on in the name of a mountain hard by a golf course which beats the brains out of most golfers. Baltusrol — the golf course — lies on land that more than 100 years ago was owned by Louis Keller, the man who founded the Social Register.

Never lacking for nerve or initiative, Keller already had nine holes and a name in place when he invited a select group of friends, no doubt all listed in his elitist publication, to join his club. At that first meeting in October 1895, Keller was named secretary, a position he would hold until his death 27 years later. The growth and vitality of Baltusrol is largely due to this enigmatic man's vision and persistence: For example, in order to facilitate the travel of his

1901 U.S. Women's Amateur. Since then, the club has played host to a national tournament almost every decade: the 1903, 1915, 1936, 1954, 1967, 1980, and 1993 U.S. Opens; the 1904, 1926, and 1946 U.S. Amateurs; the 1911 U.S. Women's Amateur; and the 1961 and 1985 U.S. Women's Opens.

The 1967 and 1980 Opens were won by Jack Nicklaus. In 1967, he set a new Open 72-hole total record of 275. As USGA executive director Joe Dey said: "The Lower course at Baltusrol is always a wonderful championship

Go Directly To Jail

The par-4 third hole at Baltusrol is considered the toughest hole on the course. At 466 yards from the blue tees or 405 from the whites, its length alone presents a challenge to any golfer. In the words of Jack Nicklaus, the third "sets up such an interesting approach. The left side of the green slopes sharply to the left. A shot from the right side of the fairway — undoubtedly with one of the mid-irons — will tend to bounce left and may run right off the green. Ideally, then, the approach should be hit from the left side of the fairway so that it will land into the slope of the green. But the left side is far more dangerous off the tee. The hole doglegs slightly from right to left, and a drive that misses the fairway to the left will be, as we say, in jail."

members from New York City to the course by rail, he purchased the New York and New Orange Railroad in 1904!

Keller's dogged determination led to Baltusrol's first national championship, the

test, and this time it was absolutely prime — wonderful lies in close-cropped fairways, putting greens that were keen and firm, and a thorough gauge of trueness of stroke...There were some wonderful individual rounds, and they only confirmed the truth that great and fair golf courses yield to great play." In 1980, the great Golden Bear was in a morass of self-doubt; the previous year he had failed to win even a single tournament for the first time in his career. But whoever invented the slogan "Jack is back!" was prophetic, as Nicklaus showed he had regained his form right from the start, just missing a three-footer on 18 to post a first-round 63. He maintained his form for the next three days, winning his fourth Open, setting a new Open scoring record of 272, and edging Isao Aoki by two shots.

Not all of these championships were played on the same golf course, for Baltusrol had expanded to 36 holes in 1922 under the brilliant, and sometimes bizarre, guidance of architect A. W. Tillinghast. "Tillie the Terrible" was a photographer, author, newspaper columnist,

The 17th is often called one of the finest par 5s in existence. At 630 yards, it has length, and cross-bunkers come into play on the second shot.

BALTUSROL GOLF CLUB
SPRINGFIELD, NEW JERSEY

HOLE	YARDAGE	PAR			
1	478	5	10	454	4
2	381	4	11	428	4
3	466	4	12	193	3
4	194	3	13	401	4
5	413	4	14	415	4
6	470	4	15	430	4
7	505	5	16	216	3
8	374	4	17	630	5
9	205	3	18	542	5
OUT	3,486	36	IN	3,709	36
			TOTAL	7,195	72

TEES	LENGTH	PAR	RATING
BLUE	7,195	72	74.9
WHITE	6,599	72	72.3
RED	5,963	75	75.8

The opening hole of the Lower course is a gem. At 478 yards, it plays as a par 5 for members and a par 4 for the pros.

architect, dilettante, spendthrift, genius. The "Creator of Baltusrol," as he billed himself, was also the designer of Winged Foot, among others. His underlying philosophy was to give birth to the "course beautiful" — a golf course in harmony with its natural setting. "It costs no more to follow Nature than to ignore her," he wrote to aspiring architects. "If you must introduce artificial creations into a golf design, take efforts to make them appear natural." It is widely recorded that Tillinghast's usual workday entailed arriving at the site in a chauffeured limousine dressed like a Wall Street banker, finding a shady spot where he would sit upon his shooting stick, sipping from a seemingly bottomless flask, and barking orders at beleaguered laborers. Prior to the 1954 Open, the club hired

Robert Trent Jones to, in his words, "make the course fairer for the average player and harder for the low handicapper." While the Lower course has gained the most notoriety, many members speak just as highly of the Upper.

The 194-yard fourth hole on Baltusrol's Lower course is considered one of the finest par 3s in golf. The club's official history recounts this anecdote about Robert Trent Jones and one of his critics who considered the remodeled fourth too difficult. "Let's go play the hole and see if there is anything that needs to be done," Jones suggested. He stepped onto the tee, drew his club back, and hit the ball into the hole for an ace! "Gentlemen," said the architect, "I think this hole is eminently fair."

——— Orlando, Florida ———

BAY HILL

Club

Architect: Dick Wilson
Opened for Play: 1961

The story of the Bay Hill Club is entangled with that of Arnold Palmer, one of the titans of the game in the 20th century. Palmer, whose hard-charging, never-say-die attitude brought golf to popular attention in the late 1950s and 1960s, redefined the game in every way and injected it with excitement. In those days, no one hit the ball quite as hard, no one made up so many shots in the late going to win tournaments (or lost as many to lose the occasional event), no one won quite so many tournaments, no one won as much money, and no one was more charismatic. Ask most any golfer who they would want in their dream foursome, and his name will most likely be mentioned more frequently than any other.

In his professional heyday, "Arnie" (like all superheroes, Palmer generally goes by one name only) won more than 90 national and international championships, including four Masters, two British Opens, a U.S. Open, and the 1955 Canadian Open (his first pro victory).

Tees	Length	Par	Rating
Palmer	7,114	72	74.6
Championship	6,586	72	71.8
Men's	6,198	72	70.2
Ladies'	5,192	72	72.3

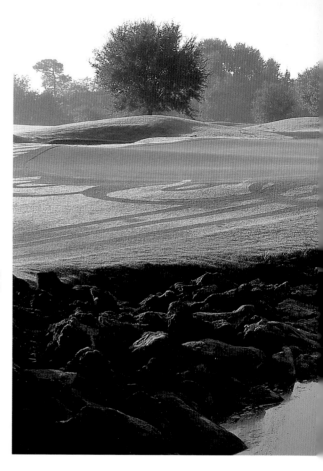

Although those glory days were long gone by the mid- to late 1990s, Palmer was still making more money than any other golfer — well over $10 million — the vast majority of it from endorsement deals from companies who still wanted their names

Bay Hill Club
Orlando, Florida

HOLE	YARDAGE	PAR			
1	441	4	10	400	4
2	218	3	11	428	4
3	395	4	12	570	5
4	530	5	13	364	4
5	365	4	14	206	3
6	543	5	15	425	4
7	197	3	16	481	5
8	424	4	17	219	3
9	467	4	18	441	4
OUT	3,580	36	IN	3,534	36
			TOTAL	7,114	72

The par-4 13th hole at Bay Hill isn't long at only 364 yards, but it compensates with lots of trouble.

From the "Palmer" tees, the par-4 eighth hole stretches 424 yards.

attached to the man who remained one of the best-known and well-respected sportsmen and businessmen in the world.

His penchant for golf courses extends beyond the normal affection most pros have for the places where they earn their living. Palmer was raised at the Latrobe Country Club in Pennsylvania where his father was the golf professional and grounds superintendent for 50 years. "Some of my earliest memories are of riding around the golf course on my father's tractor," Palmer recalls. "When I was three, he made a special set of golf clubs for me and taught me how to hold them." The psychological pressure which eventually led to him purchasing Bay Hill might be revealed by a quote he made about those days at Latrobe, when he was prohibited from playing the course except in the very early morning or at dusk, and when the clubhouse and other amenities were off limits. "It was frustrating," he reminisced. "I was raised in a country club atmosphere but was unable to touch it. It was like looking at a piece of cake and knowing how good it was but not being able to take a bite."

His "cake" came along in the mid-1960s when he played an exhibition with Jack Nicklaus at Bay Hill in Orlando, Florida, a tough, young layout by Dick Wilson, and fell in love with the course. Wilson was considered the patriarch of course design in Florida, after learning the craft from William Flynn (Shinnecock, Cherry Hills, Cascades, etc.). Starting with the West Palm Beach Country Club in 1949, he built an admirable portfolio of excellent courses in addition to Bay Hill, including the original 36 holes at Doral and extensive renovations at Seminole. He rarely ventured north, but when he did he created fine layouts such as

The par-3 second hole demands a mid- or long-iron shot to a tough green.

An "Impossible" Finish

The final two holes at Bay Hill have been called "impossible" — and much, much worse — by PGA Tour pros who visit here each season. After hopefully surviving the 17th (perhaps the toughest par 3 on Tour), the 18th presents a myriad of opportunities to make bogey — and much, much worse! This hole represents one of the most significant changes Arnold Palmer made when he took over the course. Lowering the green almost to the level of the pond which abuts it meant that missing the putting surface long or to the left meant blasting out of a bunker back toward the water. Altogether just what Arnie wanted: a super-tough finishing hole to reward a gambling, go-for-broke approach.

Cog Hill in Illinois, National Cash Register CC in Ohio, and Royal Montreal in Canada.

Wilson's original 18 wended through an orange grove near the Butler chain of freshwater lakes and provided a test for even the best golfers. Despite that, after purchasing the course in the 1970s, Palmer's intention was to "raise the bar" for the PGA Tour pros who visit every spring for the Bay Hill Invitational, adding hazards, lengthening tees, and bringing more water into play. An accomplished architect in his own right, he directed this fine-tuning himself, with mixed results. He won the event in 1971 with a four-round total of 270, but in 1983, he hit two balls into the water on the par-5 sixth hole, registering a 10

The 17th hole is a long and challenging par 3 that Arnold Palmer calls one of his all-time favorites.

en route to an 85, his highest total as a professional. Visitors and members now can play 27 holes: the original 18 and the Charger nine arranged as separate nine-hole layouts. The design features of the new nine approximate those of the Wilson-originated 18.

The final two holes at Bay Hill provoke the most comment: a 219-yard par 3, which Palmer calls one of his all-time favorites, and the par-4 18th, a 441-yard dogleg, featuring water, sand, and trees. The 17th is frequently ranked as one of the most difficult holes on the PGA Tour, with its green protected by water and many treacherous pin positions. The 18th has been called "unfair" (among other, unprintable adjectives) and has been ranked in the past as the toughest hole on Tour, based on the players' stroke averages. Many players simply bite the bullet and lay up on their second shot, sacrificing macho for a chance to make par.

The lodge at the Bay Hill Club hearkens back to a time when private clubs offered comfortable on-site accommodations for visiting guests. This tradition is still very much a part of the Bay Hill tradition, where guests are treated as club members during their stay. The two lodge buildings offer a total of 58 rooms. The lodge represents an ideal hideaway for a business meeting, family vacation, or golf getaway. Tennis courts, swimming, and a marina round out the amenities.

The par-5 16th hole is the No. 2 stroke hole on the Cascades course at The Homestead. Just over 520 yards from the tips, it confounds most players with a demanding tee shot threatened by bunkers and then, for those gutsy enough to go for the green in two, water which laps at the very edge of the putting surface.

————— *Hot Springs, Virginia* —————

THE CASCADES

Golf Course

Architect: William S. Flynn
Opened for Play: 1924

The Homestead, Virginia's famed luxury resort founded in 1766, is home to the Cascades — an award-winning William Flynn design — often referred to as America's finest mountain course. Although the resort also showcases two other distinctive 18-hole championship courses, The Homestead (1892) and Lower Cascades (1962), designed by Donald Ross and Robert Trent Jones respectively, it is to the Cascades that the accolades have gone since its opening in 1924.

The Cascades has been ranked as high as 39th in the U.S. on *Golf Digest*'s list and 43rd in America and 76th in the world by *Golf* magazine. It has also been selected as the No. 1 course in the state by *Golf Digest, Golf, and Golfweek*. More significantly, perhaps, it has been recognized as the third-best public-access course in the

The 192-yard, par-3 18th hole is an unusual but exciting finish to a round on The Homestead's Cascades course.

Just Don't Miss

At 476 yards, the par-4 12th hole is considered by most to be the Cascades' toughest obstacle. The undulating fairway, lined on both sides by trees, further threatens a tee shot with a stream, which outlines its left boundary, and a mountain on the right. "There's not a lot of 'miss' on this hole," says Director of Golf Wayne Nooe. About 100 yards out from the green, crossbunkers signal an interruption to the fairway. The green is deep and well bunkered.

country behind only Pinehurst No. 2 and Pebble Beach.

Nestled in the majestic Allegheny Mountains, The Homestead resort and its three courses boast a rich heritage as the South's ultimate haven for grooming the likes of past and present PGA Tour stars. Sam Snead began his professional career there in 1934, and The Homestead's touring professional Lanny Wadkins, a native of Virginia, captured the 1970 Virginia State Amateur Championship on the Cascades course.

"There isn't any kind of hill you don't have to play from or any kind of shot you won't hit there," says Snead. "If you could train a youngster to play on that course, he'll be able to play anywhere."

Through the years, the Cascades has played host to numerous well-known tournaments, such as the 1928 U.S. Women's Amateur, 1966 Curtis Cup, 1967 U.S. Women's Open, 1980 U.S. Senior, 1988 U.S. Amateur, 1994 U.S. Women's Amateur, and

1995 Merrill Lynch Senior PGA Tour Shoot-Out Championship.

The 6,566-yard, par-70 Cascades is noted for its long, narrow fairways, fast greens, and mountainous routing which takes it through the headwaters of the Cascades Stream and its 12 spectacular waterfalls. "You must keep the ball in the fairway on this course," says Director of Golf Wayne Nooe. "There is a real premium on accuracy, and once you get to the greens, you'll find they are quick and difficult to read. When you're over a putt, especially the short ones, the slopes from the surrounding mountains are in your peripheral vision, and that can throw you off." Nooe says that

first-time visitors who look at the scorecard and judge the Cascades by its yardage are in for a surprise. "We have five par 3s and one par 4 under 300 yards, so the remaining 12 holes are long."

Although the 12th is the toughest hole, Nooe likes the unique challenge presented by the par-5 16th: "It's only 525 yards long, and

THE CASCADES GOLF COURSE
HOT SPRINGS, VIRGINIA

HOLE	YARDAGE	PAR			
1	394	4	10	375	4
2	412	4	11	191	3
3	283	4	12	476	4
4	198	3	13	438	4
5	576	5	14	408	4
6	369	4	15	222	3
7	425	4	16	525	5
8	141	3	17	491	5
9	450	4	18	192	3
OUT	3,248	35	IN	3,318	35
			TOTAL	6,566	70

TEES	LENGTH	PAR	RATING
BLUE	6,566	70	72.9
WHITE	6,282	70	71.6
RED	5,448	71	72.9

Short at 491 yards, the par-5 17th compensates by threatening the player with water, bunkers, and inhospitable forest.

the long hitters can cut the corner leaving them with about 220 into the green. The waters of the Cascades Stream come right up to the fringe of the green, on the same level as the putting surface. It's very unusual." In addition to threatening the approach shot, the stream can come into play throughout the hole as it delineates the right border of the hole before cutting across the fairway in front of the green.

The Lower Cascades course is a 6,633-yard, par-72 layout with large greens and rolling fairways. The 6,211-yard, par-72 Homestead course boasts the oldest first tee still in continuous use in the United States. It opened in 1892 as a six-hole track and was expanded to 18 in 1913.

In 1994, under the direction of Dallas-based Club Resorts Inc., The Homestead course received more than $1 million in upgrades, a part of a multimillion dollar restoration plan for the resort. All redesign work was overseen by architect Rees Jones and included new bunkers and tees and the relocation of the 18th hole. A new driving range was added adjacent to The Homestead course which features The Homestead Golf Advantage School, a renowned teaching facility. Club Resorts Inc., a subsidiary of Club Corporation of America, also owns and operates such prestigious destinations as Pinehurst Resort and Country Club in North Carolina, Barton Creek in Texas, Quail Hollow Resort and Country Club in Ohio, and Mont Ste-Anne in Quebec, Canada.

Club Resorts' slogan is "Where every guest is a member." At Homestead, that boast is not an idle one. Founded more than 230 years ago, The Homestead built its reputation upon the hot mineral springs which were reputed to restore health and vitality. The men's bathhouse, the oldest spa structure in America and used by Thomas Jefferson, was constructed in 1761. In 1890,

M. E. Ingalls formed a syndicate to acquire the 15,000 acres and transform them into a complete resort. Four generations of Ingalls headed the development of The Homestead until 1993.

In that period, notables such as Henry Ford, Thomas Edison, John D. Rockefeller Sr., New York mayor Jimmy Walker, heavyweight Gene Tunney, and more than a dozen presidents have enjoyed the resort's facilities. Today, in addition to the spa, hot springs, and golf, guests enjoy skiing, ice skating, shooting, tennis, equestrian activities, trout fishing, mountain biking, hiking, and more.

The dogleg-left 13th is a long par 4 with cross-bunkers staggered across the fairway.

Houston, Texas

CHAMPIONS

Golf Club

Architect: Ralph Plummer
Opened for Play: 1959

When it came to building their golf course, former Tour players Jimmy Demaret (it's redundant to call him "colorful") and Jack Burke Jr. thought like the Texans they were. "We wanted a club right in our hometown that would be to Houston what Augusta National is to Georgia, what Pinehurst is to North Carolina, and what Pebble Beach is to the California coastline," said Demaret. They succeeded with the Champions: It is big, bold, and brash, just like Texas.

Although they employed a local course architect, Ralph Plummer, and were intelligent enough to defer to him where appropriate, Demaret and Burke left their stamp all over the Champions. Both were "champions" in their own right: Demaret, in addition to numerous PGA Tour wins, was the first three-time Masters champ;

At 460 yards from the back tees, and with a strategically placed fairway bunker, water, and more sand greenside, the 11th hole is an extremely tough par 4.

Burke's titles included a Masters and a PGA Championship. Both played in four Ryder Cups. The story goes that their input into Champions consisted of hitting shot after shot into projected green sites to ensure the hole would play as they wished.

Since the first tee was stuck in the ground on the Plummer-designed Cypress Creek course, Champions has been known as a "player's course." A large proportion of the membership boast single-digit handicaps. The

founders wanted it that way, but they didn't make it an easy accomplishment: The par-71 layout plays to more than 7,100 yards from the tips. More than 70,000 trees line its wide fairways and surround its huge greens. As a trade-off, there are relatively few bunkers.

When Demaret and Burke called upon George Fazio to design a course complementary to the Cypress Creek track, he gave them the par-72, 7,000-yard Jackrabbit course in 1964. Both courses have distinct personalities — while

Cypress Creek is a sprawling layout, Jackrabbit is tighter with smaller, contoured greens. But it is generally the older course to which golfers refer when they mention "Champions."

The Cypress Creek course at Champions first gained acclaim as the site of the 1967 Ryder Cup where Ben Hogan captained a high-powered squad composed of Julius Boros, Gay Brewer, Billy Casper, Gardner Dickinson, Al Geiberger, Gene Littler, Bobby Nichols, Arnold Palmer, Johnny Pott, and Doug Sanders. Needless to say, the Americans won going away.

Encouraged by rave reviews stemming from the Ryder Cup players, the United States Golf Association selected Champions as the site of the 1969 U.S. Open. Former U.S. Army sergeant Orville Moody won the event with a one-over-par total of 281, edging Bob Rosburg, Geiberger, and future PGA Tour commissioner Deane Beman by a single shot.

Except for that year in 1969, Champions had been the regular host of the PGA Tour

stop in Houston. Arnold Palmer won the inaugural Houston Champions International in 1966 — after a rain delay that lasted six months and 10 days! The event, which was scheduled for May, was rained out and replayed in November. In 1967, Frank Beard denied Palmer the chance to repeat by a shot. The 1968 tournament had bittersweet overtones as Roberto de Vicenzo won by a stroke over Lee Trevino. This came only weeks after de Vicenzo had been disqualified from the Masters due to a scoring error by Bob Goalby. Gibby Gilbert won in 1970 and Hubert Green in 1971.

CHAMPIONS GOLF CLUB HOUSTON, TEXAS CYPRESS CREEK COURSE

HOLE	YARDAGE	PAR			
1	455	4	10	453	4
2	450	4	11	460	4
3	425	4	12	213	3
4	221	3	13	530	5
5	514	5	14	431	4
6	424	4	15	416	4
7	431	4	16	181	3
8	186	3	17	448	4
9	512	5	18	440	4
OUT	3,618	36	IN	3,572	35
			TOTAL	7,190	71

TEES	LENGTH	PAR
BACK	7,190	71
MIDDLE	6,513	71
FORWARD	5,607	71

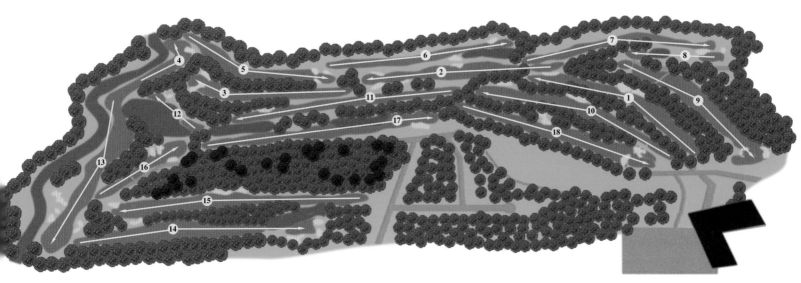

FROM LEFT: Jerry Lewis, Jack Burke, Bob Hope, Jimmy Demaret, and Mickey Mantle. Occasionally friends dropped in to see Burke and Demaret at Champions.

Jimmy And Jack — True Champions

While many modern golfers look at the Champions Golf Club as the lasting legacy of Jimmy Demaret and Jack Burke Jr., their individual competitive records stand on their own. Demaret, renowned for his sartorial excesses, was born in Houston in 1910 and learned his golf from Jack Burke Sr. Between 1935 and 1955, he won more than 70 tournaments, finishing in the money in over 325 events. He won the Masters in 1940, 1947, and 1950 and was named one of the 10 outstanding golfers of the first half of the 20th century by his admirers in the PGA and the press. Burke, with his leading-man looks, might have made a bigger impact had he not served in the marines for four years as a judo instructor. Upon his return, it was golf courses he wrestled into submission. During his first year on Tour, he won four events. In 1951, he won four events in 21 days. In his 10 years on Tour, he won the Masters, the PGA Championship, the Japan Open, and 13 other events.

Nothing tests a player's mettle like a long-iron carry over water to a tricky green. The par-3 12th at the Champions is a good example.

The 13th is not an overly long par 5 at 530 yards, but it requires two precise shots to offer the player an eagle putt. Beware the overhanging trees and greenside bunkers.

That final version in 1971 of the Houston Champions International had a pall cast over it for all time when it became known for the calamity that finally ended Hogan's competitive career. On the 220-yard fourth hole, the 59-year-old Hogan hooked three tee shots into the ravine that guards the left side. Descending into the abyss to determine if the last shot was playable, Hogan slipped, twisting the same knee that he seriously injured in the auto accident that nearly claimed his life 20 years earlier. He made a nine on the hole and eventually called for a cart to take him to the clubhouse on the 11th hole, saying to spectators as he departed: "Don't ever get old."

After extensive renovations to the Cypress Creek course, Champions returned to the PGA Tour schedule in 1990 when it played host to the Tour Championship. Jodie Mudd defeated Billy Mayfair on the first extra hole to claim what was then professional golf's largest purse: $450,000. The 1993 U.S. Amateur was played on both the Cypress Creek and Jackrabbit courses.

The par-3 12th hole at Cherry Hills demands a precise short- or mid-iron shot over water to a subtle green.

— Englewood, Colorado —

CHERRY HILLS

Country Club

Architect: William Flynn
Opened for Play: 1923

Cherry Hills Country Club is a storied course near Denver which, despite its location, is not a typical mountain course. The rolling, well-treed William Flynn layout has played host to nine significant national championships: U.S. Opens in 1938, 1960, and 1978; PGA Championships in 1941 and 1985; the 1993 U.S. Senior Open; the 1976 U.S. Senior Amateur; the 1983 U.S. Mid-Amateur; and the 1990 U.S. Amateur.

Architect Flynn, an accomplished player who had competed against Francis Ouimet in high school in Massachusetts, came to the attention of the golfing world on the basis of his fine work as Hugh Wilson's assistant at Merion. Most notable among his design work is Shinnecock Hills in New York; his reputation was such that he also was invited to renovate such famous courses as Pine Valley

An island green provides the final challenge at the 555-yard, par-5 17th hole.

in New Jersey and The Country Club in Massachusetts. Although his name is most commonly linked with Howard Toomey, his partner for several years, he was also responsible for launching the careers of architects William Gordon, Dick Wilson, and Robert Lawrence. Flynn's original work at Cherry Hills has been altered over the years by Press Maxwell as well as Arnold Palmer and his sidekick Ed Seay.

Palmer's involvement extends far beyond his renovation work, for Cherry Hills stakes much of its notoriety on Arnie's antics here during the 1960 U.S. Open; perhaps the reverse is also true. Indeed, this Open remains significant as the one where three generations of superstars realigned golf's hierarchy. Palmer had won his first Tour event five years earlier and was the darling of not only Arnie's Army, but all golfers; Ben Hogan was gearing down from a Hall of Fame career; and a crew-cut kid from Columbus, Ohio, named Jack Nicklaus, was giving notice that he would be a factor in the future.

Seven shots back of the leader, Mike Souchak, on the final day, Palmer immediately electrified the crowd by driving the 404-yard first hole and making birdie. No doubt his natural power was aided by Cherry Hills' mile-high altitude, but it also got an undisputed assist from an old friend of Palmer's, sportswriter Bob Drum. Prior to the last round, Drum informed Palmer that he might as well coast in because he was too far back to catch Souchak. "Well, the way I read it is that a 65 would give me 280 for the tournament, and 280 is the kind of score that usually wins the U.S. Open," Palmer responded with a dangerous glint in his eye.

Although no one (with the possible exception of Arnie himself) realized it at the time, that first tee shot signaled the demise of Souchak and the other 13 golfers who were between Palmer and first place. Palmer wasn't thinking that he had made double-bogey,

CHERRY HILLS COUNTRY CLUB
ENGLEWOOD, COLORADO

HOLE	YARDAGE	PAR			
1	404	4	10	445	4
2	421	4	11	577	5
3	328	4	12	207	3
4	437	4	13	387	4
5	543	5	14	480	4
6	171	3	15	215	3
7	394	4	16	433	4
8	234	3	17	555	5
9	438	4	18	491	5
OUT	3,370	35	IN	3,790	37
			TOTAL	7,160	72

TEES	LENGTH	PAR	RATING
GOLD	7,160	72	73.8
BLUE	6,872	72	72.4
WHITE	6,481	72	70.4
RED	5,851	74	74.3

bogey, and par here in the first three rounds; *Go For Broke!* was more than the title of his autobiography, it was a characteristic as engrained in the man as his infectious smile and natural charisma. What was he thinking standing on the first tee of Cherry Hills, knowing he had to fire a six-under-par score that day to have even a chance of winning the Open? One only has to look at the quotation from Scottish poet Alexander Smith which prefaces his book: "Everything is sweetened by risk." This round would define Palmer's career: "I'd shown that my idea did work — that boldness could conquer this hole," he wrote later. "And that if it made the first hole yield, then the whole course could be conquered with boldness."

He chipped in on the second hole, birdied the third, dropped a twisting 40-foot putt to birdie the fourth, parred the fifth, birdied the sixth and seventh. He made the turn at 30, tied with Souchak, and took the lead two holes later. It was, in the words of revered golf writer Herbert Warren Wind, "the most explosive stretch of sub-par golf any golfer has ever produced in the championship." It was also the basis of his 65 for the day, enough for the 280 total he had prophesied. He would go on to win 32 tournaments in the next three years and become golf's first million-dollar man.

Like many remarkable par 4s, the 13th at Cherry Hills puts the emphasis on shaping the tee shot and then picking the perfect club for the approach to a protected green.

On the way to claiming the trophy, Palmer passed Hogan who, although on the back nine of a marvelous career, was still in contention to win his fifth Open. Alas, Hogan's approach shot at 17 found the water, leading to a bogey, and another water shot on 18 gave him a 73. Palmer also edged Nicklaus who finished two shots back, the best finish by an amateur in the national Open since Johnny Goodman won the tournament in 1933.

The first hole at Cherry Hills has it all: great design, a spectacular view, and a unique place in golf history.

"The Maddening First Hole"

In his autobiography, *Go For Broke!*, Arnold Palmer recounts how the first hole of Cherry Hills Country Club was pivotal not only in his eventually winning the

1960 U.S. Open, but also how it defined the rest of his stellar career: "...it was not until the U.S. Open at Cherry Hills that I put it all together, philosophically as well as physically. For not until that summer day in 1960 did it become apparent to me how boldness might influence not just a hole but an entire round, an entire tournament, and even an entire golfing career." Despite the fact that he was three over par on this hole for the tournament, Palmer did not hesitate in pulling his driver out of the bag and smashing the ball with every ounce of his being. "The ball went up and hung in the sharp, clear air as if it had been painted there. When it came down — with overspin — it leaped forward and ran through the rough and right onto the middle of the green."

Ironically, Palmer returned as a course architect in the mid-1970s, and one of the changes he made was to stretch the championship tee on that first hole back another 50 yards!

The par-4 ninth at Colonial Country Club is less than 400 yards long, but the approach shot must carry a pond on its way to a two-tiered green.

————— *Fort Worth, Texas* —————

COLONIAL

Country Club

Architect: John Bredemus
Opened for Play: 1936

Credit probably wasn't something that Marvin Leonard was very fond of. As a merchant in pre-WWII Fort Worth, cash was preferred. But there is no question that all the credit for the Colonial Country Club goes directly to this visionary.

Did Leonard foresee the club playing host to the 1941 U.S. Open, the first Open to be held in a Southern state? No. Did he gaze into the future and determine that the Colonial National Invitation Tournament would become one of the most prestigious events in professional golf? Doubtful. All Leonard really wanted in the first place was a golf course with bent grass greens.

In the mid-1930s, unable to persuade any of the existing local facilities to convert from Bermuda grass to bent, Leonard decided he would build his own. He contracted Texas course designer John

Bredemus and set him and foreman Ralph Plummer loose on 158 acres of heavy clay bottom land along the Clear Fork of the Trinity River bristling with pecan trees, hackberry bushes, sycamores, and oaks.

"John could actually see the greens and tees," said another famed Texan named Harvey Penick, recalling when they walked the property. "All I could see was knee-deep grass, brush, and chiggers crawling up my pants leg." Bredemus overcame the natural hazards as well as Leonard's intransigence on some issues, and then issued the following advice to Penick, who would make his name in golf instruction: "If they ever ask you to build a course, do the best job you can with the money they give you, then leave town. Because you can never please all golfers." Despite those comments, the result pleased most who visited there. Cary Middlecoff, 1951 Colonial winner, calls it the toughest par 70 in the world.

Bredemus deserves a mention not only because of the quality of his work, but also

COLONIAL COUNTRY CLUB
FORT WORTH, TEXAS

HOLE	YARDAGE	PAR		HOLE	YARDAGE	PAR
1	565	5		10	404	4
2	400	4		11	599	5
3	476	4		12	433	4
4	246	3		13	178	3
5	459	4		14	426	4
6	393	4		15	430	4
7	420	4		16	188	3
8	192	3		17	383	4
9	391	4		18	427	4
OUT	3,542	35		IN	3,468	35
				TOTAL	7,010	70

because he was a loner who, it has been written, "came to be known as a tax-dodging, shoeless eccentric who ate nothing but vanilla wafers and played a mean game of checkers." While there may be elements of truth in that statement, it is definitely known that Bredemus was an Olympic track and field athlete who worked as a school principal prior to becoming a mediocre pro golfer in 1919. In all, he would design about 50 courses in his home state prior to a disagreement with the Internal Revenue Service in the late 1930s which led to a self-imposed exile to Mexico until his death in 1946.

Although Bredemus is the architect of record, another man perhaps has had more impact on the modern reputation of Colonial's design. Determined to impress the United States Golf Association and the world's finest players prior to the 1941 Open, Leonard purchased additional acreage and hired Perry Maxwell to build three holes to replace the existing third, fourth, and fifth. Maxwell, who was famed for designing Prairie Dunes in Kansas and Southern Hills in Oklahoma, had a well-deserved reputation for the sadistic greens he contoured at courses such as Augusta National and Pine Valley. The result exceeded even his fiendish intentions, with the three holes being

Excellent bunkering combines with superbly conditioned greens to create some interesting targets.

renowned as the "Horrible Horseshoe." With assistance from Dean Woods, Maxwell created the excruciatingly difficult fifth, known far and wide as "Death Valley." They lengthened the third hole by some 50 yards and pumped up the par-3 fourth to almost 250 yards.

Reigning Masters champion Craig Wood would win the 1941 Open, wearing a brace to support a back injured in a serious car accident. His victory came at the expense of two of Fort Worth's favorite sons: Byron Nelson and Ben Hogan. Indeed, Colonial would soon acquire the nickname "Hogan's Alley,"

reflecting both Hogan's affection for the club and the narrowness of the course itself.

That Open simply whetted Leonard's appetite for a big event. He realized what the Masters had done for Augusta, Georgia, and he thought his hometown deserved no less. He drummed up support for the first Colonial NIT in 1946 and dug deep for a purse of $15,000, the third-largest on Tour at the time. The ending to the script was perfect as local hero Ben Hogan claimed the winner's share of $3,000. Hogan successfully defended his title in 1947 and won the event five times in total.

Hogan's performance brought Leonard's vision full circle. For it was the Fort Worth merchant who had shelled out a few dollars in the 1920s to send Hogan out on Tour, starting a personal and business relationship that would last until Leonard's death in 1970.

Hogan's professional achievements garnered him many accolades, but he placed great value on his relationship with Leonard and Colonial, which houses the impressive and popular Ben Hogan Trophy Room. In one of his last significant interviews a few years ago, an emotional Hogan declared: "That's why we have this trophy room over at Colonial right now, because they're his [Leonard's]. Without him I couldn't have done it."

The Horrible Horseshoe

The third, fourth, and fifth holes at Colonial Country Club are known as the "Horrible Horseshoe," not only for their configuration, but for their impact on your score. Former director of golf Roland Harper calls the fifth hole "Colonial's calling card... It's everything that's been said about it and more. You have to fade your tee shot with a 3-wood (few have the courage to hit a driver here) into a narrow landing area, and you're still left with a 200-yard plus shot. Cut the shot too much and you're in the Trinity River; play a draw and leave it out and you're in the Trinity River; hit too big a draw and you're in a ditch on the left. The green has two tiers and a bunker guarding it on both the left and right. Take a par here anytime you can get it."

Often cited as the toughest green on the course, the 16th slopes downhill from right to left, making a nightmare of any putt from above the hole.

—— Pebble Beach, California ——

CYPRESS POINT

Golf Club

Architect: Alister Mackenzie
Opened for Play: 1928

In a classic case of the "rich get richer," Cypress Point combined with Spyglass Hill and Pebble Beach to create a triumvirate of golf unmatched anywhere. Golf in the Monterey Peninsula, perhaps the most pleasant place to visit in the world, is by no means limited to the "Big Three," but it is most certainly dominated by them. In contrast to its public neighbors, Cypress Point is very private. Although the AT&T Pebble Beach National Pro-Am used to be played on the three courses, Poppy Hills has supplanted Cypress as the third venue. Other than that, the 1981 Walker Cup was the last significant tournament played at Cypress Point, and that suits the members just fine.

By 1928, Alister Mackenzie, an Englishman whose insights on course architecture provided a legacy which remains to this day, had

The par-5 sixth, at 518 yards, is reachable by better players in two strokes.

done a little work in the United States. Overshadowed to that point, Mackenzie rocketed to international prominence with the inspired Cypress Point Golf Club. Granted, he was blessed with a tremendous piece of property upon which to work his magic. Although this site did not have the awe-inspiring dunes and cliffs of nearby Pebble Beach Golf Links, it did marry just enough of the savage Northern Californian coastline with ancient forest and rolling heathland. The result more than holds its own with any golf course in the world, despite its relatively short 6,506-yard length.

Like Pebble Beach, Cypress Point eases the player into his round, but any hole here is bound to punish the unwary or foolhardy. Although the layout is renowned for two holes of unmatched beauty and challenge, this is not a two-hole golf course. The first hole is a 418-yard par 4 from the back tees which can just as easily deliver a double-bogey as a par should you stray from the fairway. Numbers 2, 5, and 6 are challenging par 5s reachable by the better player in two strokes while the seventh hole is a pretty mid-length par 3 played across a valley. Woods surround you after leaving the second green, and you meander through them for the next eight holes.

The astute golfer will begin the round cautiously in order to stand on the eighth tee at or under par. The scorecard definitely does not tell the tale about the final two holes of the front nine. These classic short par 4s require precise tee shots — leave the driver in the bag — in order to set up a short pitch to elevated greens surrounded by sand. Sand, ice plants, trees, and Mackenzie's inspired design conspire to ensure you leave the front nine well over par. On No. 11, you head back

A breathtaking par 4, the 18th at Cypress Point is a fitting conclusion to a round at Alister Mackenzie's masterpiece.

CYPRESS POINT GOLF CLUB
PEBBLE BEACH, CALIFORNIA

HOLE	YARDAGE	PAR			
1	418	4	10	491	5
2	551	5	11	434	4
3	161	3	12	409	4
4	385	4	13	362	4
5	491	5	14	383	4
6	522	5	15	139	3
7	163	3	16	233	3
8	355	4	17	376	4
9	291	4	18	342	4
OUT	3,337	37	IN	3,169	35
			TOTAL	6,506	72

Pity Poor Porky!

Playing the 16th hole in the 1953 Bing Crosby Pro-Am (the precursor to the AT&T), Porky Oliver smacked five consecutive balls into the Pacific. Although past his prime, Oliver was still a competent touring pro. His sixth shot stayed dry, albeit in the rough, and the final result was a 13-over-par 16! On the other hand, Jerry Pate aced this hole in the 1982 Crosby, and tournament patriarch Bing did the same thing in the event's very first visit to Cypress Point in 1947.

toward the rocky peninsula, playing close to the ocean on a couple of holes before reaching the climax of your round.

While every hole at Cypress Point is a joy, it is the 16th and 17th holes that are Cypress Point in most golfers' minds. After enjoying the short par-3 15th, which begins the course's flirtation with the ocean, the first-time player steps onto a tee from which, he swears, he has played before. This is Cypress Point's spectacular 16th, perhaps the most photographed hole in golf. Now, *this* is a par 3! More than 230 yards of carry over a finger of the Pacific to a green set on a precipitous peninsula; while there is a bailout area to the left, what self-respecting golfer could ignore one of golf's ultimate challenges?

The Golf Course, the definitive book by Geoffrey Cornish and Ron Whitten, offers some expert and insightful comments about this dynamic hole. The authors say it "graphically demonstrates the strategic philosophy of golf design at its heroic extreme...The cautious golfer plays short to dry land on the left, and then pitches to the green with hope of putting out for par. Without the alternative, Cypress Point's 16th would have been a terribly penal hole, unreachable to all but a few strong golfers; with it, the 16th requires a player to choose his route before swinging."

In contrast to 16, length is not the determining factor on 17, although it creates a similar course management crisis. At 376 yards, this dogleg par 4 offers a tee shot over the same Pacific inlet featured on No. 16. The gamble, of course, is to flirt with the danger and try to cut off as much of the dogleg as possible. Overestimate your ability and pay the price. Assuming you have ended up on dry land after airmailing the craggy boulders and crashing surf, you may be stymied by a stand of weather-beaten, gnarled cypress trees which looms out into the fairway about 250 yards off the tee. The right-hand side of the green teeters out into the Pacific while an hourglass-shaped bunker sits short and left. Another bunker awaits at the rear of the putting surface.

The 139-yard 15th hole brings you back to the closing holes skirting the Pacific Ocean.

An 80-foot-long bunker guarding a tiny green awaits any shot fortunate enough to carry the salt marsh on Harbour Town's par-3 17th hole.

—— Hilton Head Island, South Carolina ——

HARBOUR TOWN

Golf Links

Architect: Pete Dye
Opened for Play: 1969

Any golf fan is familiar with at least the two finishing holes at Harbour Town Golf Links, the site of the PGA Tour's MCI Heritage Classic. The par-3 17th demands a carry over water of between 176 and 192 yards for the pros to a hostile green jealously protected by an 80-foot-long bunker. The final hole is a par 4 almost 480 yards in length which provides much of the same spectacular challenge as its counterpart at Pebble Beach. Vast salt marshes and the waters of Calibogue Sound alternately border and intrude along the left side of the fairway. The tee shot must be long and accurate, yet many of the Tour's best leave the driver in the bag on this hole and use a 3-wood or 1-iron to ensure a dry result. The green, reachable on the third shot for most mortals, is hugged by water and bunkers.

The 14th is another of Pete Dye's masterful par 3s, featuring timber bulkheads, one of his trademarks.

its credit, however, Harbour Town Golf Links has become synonymous with Hilton Head Island in the minds of golfers around the world, not only for its playing experience but also for its distinctive appearance.

Harbour Town "is rightly famous among American courses for marking a turning point in the history of golf architecture, away from the Trent Jones school to the Pete Dye school," says Tom Doak in *The Confidential Guide to Golf Courses*. To be sure, this course brought a couple of Dye's design trademarks to widespread public attention: vast sandy waste areas and the railway tie bulkheads he had appropriated from ancient links courses on the other side of the Atlantic. Assisting him as a consultant, Dye had a relatively decent player who would develop into a reputable designer in his own right a few years later: Jack Nicklaus.

Measuring just over 6,900 yards from the back tees, Harbour Town is not considered long by modern Tour standards. And at 6,119 yards from the men's tees and 5,019 from the women's, this course will frighten no one who judges it by length. The deception here is that the long hitter can score well; nothing could be further from the truth, for Harbour Town demands the ultimate in course management, well-positioned shots, and accurate approaches to small greens. The course has been sculpted from more than 300 acres of live oaks, pines, and magnolias, and those towering trees have tormented golfers since Harbour Town opened in 1969. The result of a drive hit to the wrong side of the fairway will be the challenge of playing the next stroke up and over some of those arboreal obstacles.

And those are only two of the 18 tremendous holes here. Called "nothing short of a work of art" by *Sports Illustrated* when it opened, Harbour Town Golf Links is indeed a remarkable experience. It is a sister course to two others at the 5,000-acre Sea Pines Resort on South Carolina's tiny Hilton Head Island: the Ocean course and the Sea Marsh course, which offer their own challenges. To

"This is a shotmaking course," says Director of Golf Cary Corbitt. "It is position-oriented, and players are rewarded for good shots and penalized for bad ones. This course honors the skills necessary to play the game well, not just the strength."

Although Harbour Town possesses some long and difficult par 4s, such as the eighth, 11th, and 18th, it is remarkable for its collection of short, demanding par 4s, often called the most challenging aspect of golf course architecture. Right from the first hole, only 414 yards for the pros and a mere 328 for amateurs, the premium is on placing each shot in anticipation of what will be demanded on the next one. The ninth, for example, is just over 330 yards and should tempt the long hitter to drive the green. The problem with that strategy is the cavernous bunker

Aim At The Lighthouse!

The 478-yard, par-4 18th hole at Harbour Town is one of golf's most scenic finishing holes. Vast salt marshes and the waters of Calibogue Sound border and intrude along the left side of the fairway. For golfers bold enough to go straight for the flag on this signature hole, a wood or long-iron aimed directly at the red-and-white striped Harbour Town lighthouse might pay off.

Precision is demanded on the visually distracting par-3 seventh hole. Many experts say Harbour Town has the best collection of par 3s in the U.S.

Harbour Town Golf Links
Hilton Head Island, South Carolina

HOLE	YARDAGE	PAR		HOLE	YARDAGE	PAR
1	414	4		10	436	4
2	505	5		11	438	4
3	411	4		12	413	4
4	198	3		13	378	4
5	535	5		14	165	3
6	419	4		15	575	5
7	180	3		16	376	4
8	466	4		17	176/192	3
9	337	4		18	478	4
OUT	3,465	36		IN	3,435/3,451	35
				TOTAL	6,900/6,916	71

that stretches in front of the putting surface. Number 13 is another shortish par 4 that can result in a quick bogey or worse: The landing area is minuscule, but it must be hit in precisely the right spot for a short-iron approach through overhanging trees to a tiny, elevated green almost completely surrounded by sand. A little more difficult than it seems from the scorecard, don't you think?

Dye also assembled a par-3 Hall of Fame at Harbour Town. They range between 165

TEES	LENGTH	PAR	RATING
HERITAGE	6,900/6,916	71	74.0
MEN'S	6,119	71	70.0
LADIES'	5,019	71	69.0

and 198 yards for the pros (138 to 161 for amateurs), yet each one features an unexpected opportunity for disaster. After two truncated par 4s separated by a straightforward par 5, the player steps onto the fourth tee, the longest par 3 on the course. All you have to do here is hit a mid-iron across water to a small green with trees on the right and sand and water on the left. Three holes later, you are faced with a short-iron shot across water and a football field-sized waste area, not to mention encroaching trees. There is more water to carry on No. 14, and you already know about the 17th.

The majority of the Tour pros who play the MCI Heritage Classic rave about this layout as do the thousands of visitors to Sea Pines Resort who play it the other 51 weeks of the year. Perhaps the most telling comment is from Nicklaus, Dye's consultant on the project, who once said: "I get angrier here than anywhere else we play." Hit it where you're not supposed to at Harbour Town Golf Links, and you may echo his words.

Pinpoint accuracy is required on the 378-yard 13th hole if you want to finish with the same ball you started with!

Don't be fooled by the yardage — only 396 yards long — the par-4 16th is extremely demanding, like everything at Hazeltine.

HAZELTINE

National Golf Club

Architect: Robert Trent Jones
Opened for Play: 1961

It has been said that Hazeltine was built to fulfill a need in that region of America for a golf course that could test the best players in the world. In 1966, only five years after it opened, it did more than test the competitors in the U.S. Women's Open: Sandra Spuzich stumbled home as the winner with a score of nine over par. The powers that be at Hazeltine continued to pit their horse against better and better competition. In 1967, it was the Minnesota Golf Classic where Lou Graham managed to get a couple of strokes under par over the four rounds.

Then Hazeltine bumped up against the big boys in the 1970 U.S. Open, although some of the world's best professionals thought the pride of Minnesota was playing dirty. Through the ensuing decades, the people at Hazeltine have covered their ears when the name "Dave

Water comes into play on both the tee shot and approach shot on No. 16.

Hill" comes up. After shooting a second-round 69 to leave him a couple of strokes back of eventual winner Tony Jacklin, Hill told a group of golf writers: "They ruined a good farm when they built this course. Plow it up and start over." Hill was not the only moaner. The origins of the players' complaints were myriad: too many blind shots, too windy, too thick a rough, just too everything. Add Hazeltine's punitive design to the United States Golf Association's sadistic course setup, and it was a recipe for disaster with Hill the designated food critic. It seemed that

Hazeltine was down for the count, despite the fact that Jacklin registered a four-round total of 281, seven shots under par. Hill was a distant second, with his runner-up check lightened a touch by a fine from the USGA for his intemperate comments about the host club.

Hazeltine was the offspring of Robert Trent Jones, arguably the best-known golf architect of all time. Love him or hate him, Jones remains a golf icon with more than 450 courses in 23 countries to his credit. Geoffrey Cornish and Ron Whitten write in *The Architects of Golf* that Jones was "never an advocate of a strictly heroic or strategic or penal course. The trend, he felt, was to courses that featured all three philosophies blended into an appropriate combination depending on whether the course was intended as a municipal operation, a resort, a private layout, or a tournament host." This from the

man whose renovations at Oakland Hills led to Ben Hogan calling the redesigned course "a monster" in public. Obviously, in the minds of the players at least, Jones had missed his self-imposed goal of making Hazeltine the ultimate "tournament host."

But extensive renovations, first in the late 1970s, led to Hazeltine being considered once again as a legitimate venue for a major tournament. The USGA was the first to venture

Tees	Length	Par	Rating
Championship	7,237	72	75.6
Blue	7,023	72	74.7
Gold	6,601	72	72.8
White	6,184	72	70.8

HAZELTINE NATIONAL GOLF CLUB
CHASKA, MINNESOTA

HOLE	YARDAGE	PAR			
1	460	4	10	412	4
2	442	4	11	560	5
3	580	5	12	432	4
4	196	3	13	205	3
5	420	4	14	360	4
6	406	4	15	595	5
7	518	5	16	396	4
8	178	3	17	186	3
9	437	4	18	454	4
OUT	3,637	36	IN	3,600	36
			TOTAL	7,237	72

Payne-ful Experience At Hazeltine

After 72 holes of regulation play at the 1991 U.S. Open, Payne Stewart and Scott Simpson were tied at six under par. Under USGA rules, they had to return on the Monday following the tournament to face each other in an 18-hole playoff. Looking like survivors of the Bataan Death March, they stood on the 16th tee with Simpson two strokes up. Despite a shaky drive, Stewart sank a long birdie putt on the treacherous par 4 while Simpson stabbed his short par putt to fall back into a tie. Simpson then bogeyed the par-3 17th, and Stewart stumbled into the scorer's tent with the win. His 75 in the playoff was the worst extra-round score in 64 years.

A 460-yard par 4 isn't every player's idea of fun — especially when it is the first hole.

back, throwing the finest women players into its jaws in the 1977 U.S. Women's Open. The results were markedly better, with Hollis Stacy posting a score of "only" four over par to claim the trophy. Three years later, Lanny Wadkins won the PGA Grand Slam of Golf with a one-under 71 for the 18-hole made-for-TV event. Next to test the waters were the "round-bellies" in the 1983 U.S. Senior Open. Winner Billy Casper could do no better than four shots over par, a la Hollis Stacy.

No wonder it took the USGA eight more years to overcome what certainly was a high level of trepidation to bring back its flagship to Hazeltine. That decision came in the wake of yet another set of renovations, this time by Rees Jones, the son of Robert Trent Jones. According to *The Architects of Golf,* the USGA and the players had to like the changes: "[Rees Jones] set new standards for clarity and playability in design. Jones preached and practiced what he termed 'definition in design.' He wanted his holes to indicate clearly to golfers how they should play them. His hazards were visible, his bunkering directional, his targets accessible, and his mounds deflected errant balls back into play." How could you not like that philosophy?

From all accounts, most of the competitors at the 1991 U.S. Open became Rees Jones fans. Payne Stewart fired rounds of 67-70-73-72 for a six-under total of 282 over Hazeltine's reworked 7,149 yards to set up a playoff with Scott Simpson, which he won.

The USGA reappeared in 1994 with its Mid-Amateur Championship which was won by Tim Jackson. Wisely, this event was match play which could be the best format for layouts like Hazeltine.

In keeping with its tradition of playing host to major events, Hazeltine will open its doors to the PGA Championship in 2002 — following yet another set of renovations, of course.

The Honors Course in Tennessee is a tribute to the spirit of the game, the determination of the club's founders, and the architectural genius of the Dye family. Pictured is the par-4 ninth hole.

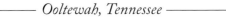

—————— Ooltewah, Tennessee ——————

THE HONORS

Course

Architects: Pete and P. B. Dye
Opened for Play: 1983

The Honors Course does just that: Its presence was intended by the developer, Jack Lupton, to honor amateur golfers. This game remains increasingly unique in the world of sports because it clearly separates the amateur from the professional. A club publication quotes the late Richard Tufts' philosophy of amateurism: "In my mind an amateur is one who competes in a sport for the joy of playing, for the companionship that it affords, for health-giving exercise, and for the relaxation from more serious matters.

As part of this lighthearted approach to the game, he accepts cheerfully all adverse breaks, is considerate of his opponent, plays the game fairly and squarely in accordance with its rules, maintains self-control, and strives to do his best, not in order to win, but rather as a test of his own skill and ability. These are his only interests, and, in them, material considerations have no part. The return which amateur sport will bring to those who play it in this spirit are greater than those any money can possibly buy."

Lupton chose an architect with more than a passing familiarity with amateur golf. Pete Dye won the Indiana Amateur in 1958 after coming second in 1954 and 1955; his wife and business partner, Alice, claimed seven Indiana Women's Amateurs, three Florida Women's Amateurs, five Women's Western Senior Amateurs, and two U.S. Women's Senior championships. In 1981, after some 20 years in the business, Dye was continuing to confound the golf world with his innovative and controversial designs. In fact, he was so liberal with the use of railway tie bulkheads that it was said he built the only golf courses that could burn down. Fortunately for traditionalists, Dye, working with his son P. B., saw fit to dispense with such artificiality at The Honors Course.

The Dyes, father and son, labored over the topographical maps to route the course through the heavily wooded Tennessee hills at the foot of White Oak Mountain. Five tee blocks on each hole guaranteed that players of every ability level would be able to enjoy The Honors experience. Fairways were drawn with the natural contour and native beauty of the

The ninth hole demonstrates how successful Pete and P. B. Dye were in integrating The Honors Course into this natural setting.

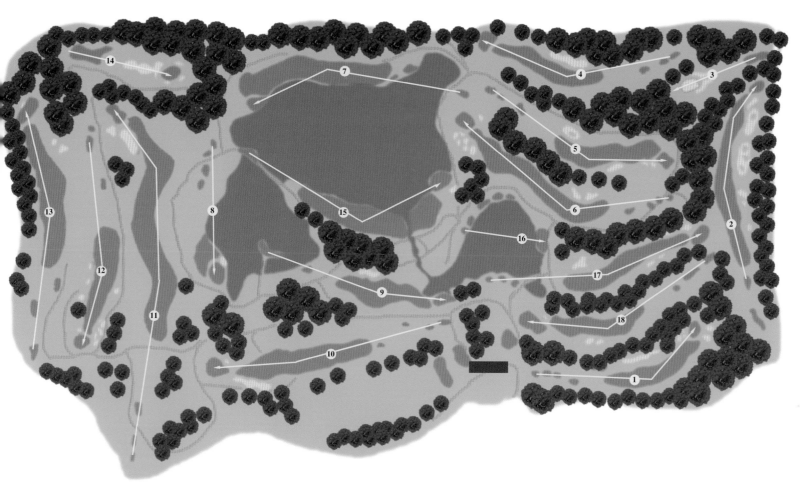

THE HONORS COURSE
OOLTEWAH, TENNESSEE

TEES	LENGTH	PAR	RATING
SILVER	7,064	72	75.4
BLUE	6,625	72	73.1
ORANGE	6,387	72	72.3
GREEN	6,131	72	71.2

HOLE	YARDAGE	PAR		HOLE	YARDAGE	PAR
1	401	4		10	435	4
2	520	5		11	562	5
3	195	3		12	355	4
4	433	4		13	394	4
5	459	4		14	156	3
6	546	5		15	443	4
7	437	4		16	208	3
8	206	3		17	494	5
9	369	4		18	451	4
OUT	3,566	36		IN	3,498	36
				TOTAL	7,064	72

land in mind. Hazards and bunkers were strategically placed, sometimes along the curving bend of a fairway, others on the underedge of an undulating green. Two lakes were located to enhance the view, to function as hazards, and to supplement other water resources. During this planning stage, Alice Dye provided vital input to make the course as playable as possible from the forward tees.

The greens, unlike the built-up greens characteristic of may new courses, meld into the existing topography. Huge mounds and bunkers of all shapes, sizes, and depths were carefully placed to enhance both the appearance and strategy of every hole. When the course opened, the Dyes were satisfied that they had created something of lasting, natural beauty. Much of the continuing credit for the reputation of The Honors Course goes to

Shadows emanate from The Honors' undulating fairways, furthering the almost mystical experience on the par-4 13th.

superintendent David Stone, "one of the nation's greatest" greenskeepers, according to Pete Dye. "He understands grass," Pete said, "and that's what makes a golf course great."

Today, as the automated front gate slowly swings open, you enter a rare and alluring world of golf. Meandering through towering pines and hardwoods, flaming azaleas and radiant dogwoods, the serene drive offers a tantalizing view of the brawny golf course. Your anticipation increases when you see fellow golfers on the expansive practice range to the left and glimpse

on the right the Guest House, a rustic two-story lodge with overnight accommodations for 16 guests. Then the clubhouse comes into view.

From the start, Jack Lupton and Alice Dye agreed on one thing: This was a golf club, not a country club. For the clubhouse, they envisioned a place where members and their guests could come for a light lunch and a relaxing afternoon of golf, topped off by a convivial atmosphere: in short, a sanctuary that would complement the character of the golf course itself.

Dedicated To Golf

While The Honors is his most publicized project, Jack Lupton should be recognized as one of the most generous golf benefactors in the United States. Lupton built his course in Ooltewah to honor amateur golf and the people who play it. Not satisfied with that contribution, Lupton again dug deep when he heard the Tennessee Golf Association was looking for funding for an exceptional project. He purchased the acreage now occupied by a building, housing most of the state's golf bodies plus an innovative short course for junior golfers which doubles as a turfgrass laboratory. The design was donated by architect Bob Cupp, and country music artist Vince Gill funded the outstanding practice facility. So successful is the short course at Aspen Grove that the Tennessee Golf Association provides plans and other materials for associations wishing to duplicate their initiative.

The hills of Tennessee provide a fiery backdrop to the exquisite and exclusive Honors Course. This is the par–4 15th hole.

Like many holes at Inverness, the par-5 13th does not overwhelm with length. This par 5 relies on precision and a small, tricky green.

INVERNESS

Club

Architect: Donald Ross
Opened for Play: 1919

Although the basic layout of Inverness with which we are familiar today is the result of Donald Ross's efforts in 1919, the history of the club actually dates back to 1903 when S. P. Jermain, the club's first president, received permission from the Scottish village of Inverness to use its name and crest.

In that year, Scottish professional Bernard Nichols laid out a nine-hole course on 78 acres which featured well-drained sandy loam soil and a brook which continues to add strategic value to Inverness. Unfortunately, Nichols would have been in trouble if he was as accurate with his golf score as he was in totaling golf holes. When construction was almost complete, it was discovered that only eight holes existed. A short hole was hurriedly sandwiched in and continued to exist until a course renovation in 1978.

The par-4 10th hole is not long but features an abundance of bunkers and a green that is very tough to read.

Tees	Length	Par	Rating
Gold	7,025	71	75.0
White	6,638	71	72.8
Blue	6,395	71	71.5
Red	5,684	74	68.5

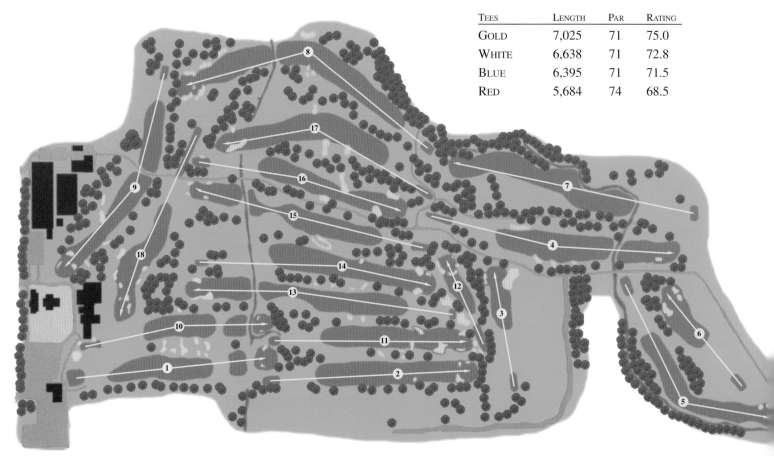

Speaking of course renovations, Inverness is almost as famed for its changes as for the number of national championships it has hosted. In addition to Ross, other architects who have been brought in to work their particular magic have included A. W. Tillinghast, Dick Wilson, Robert Bruce Harris, Arthur Hills, George Fazio, Tom Fazio, and Steve Forrest. Despite — perhaps because of — this persistent tinkering, Inverness has flourished into one of the great shotmaker's courses in the world, a compact course with fast, tiny greens which are excruciatingly difficult to read.

The history of Inverness is intertwined with the U.S. Opens it has played host to, beginning in 1920, the year after the Donald Ross masterpiece opened. The fiery long-hitter Ted Ray of England won this event which also marked the Open debut of two 18-year-olds: Robert T. Jones and Gene Sarazen. After 72 holes, Ray stood at 11-over-par 295, one shot better than Leo Diegel, Jock Hutchinson, Jack Burke, and Harry Vardon. Sadly, Vardon, well past his prime, had a five-shot lead with seven holes to go when a gale struck the golf course. The driving winds and

A Great Professional

In 1940, Inverness matched the caliber of its club professional with the reputation of the course itself. None other than Byron Nelson joined the club just after winning the 1939 U.S. Open. His record of an incredible 11 straight PGA tournament wins in 1945 still stands.

rain overwhelmed the aging Vardon while the powerfully built Ray bulled his way through the storm to claim the title.

This Open also marked the first time golf pros were allowed free access to a clubhouse; prior to that, the clubhouse was the exclusive enclave of members and their guests. The pros were so impressed by this democratic gesture that they took up a collection and purchased a massive grandfather clock which still dominates the main lobby at Inverness.

The 1931 U.S. Open was also significant because it was the longest major championship ever held, requiring 144 holes to

INVERNESS CLUB
TOLEDO, OHIO

HOLE	YARDAGE	PAR			
1	398	4	10	363	4
2	385	4	11	378	4
3	194	3	12	170	3
4	466	4	13	515	5
5	409	4	14	448	4
6	210	3	15	465	4
7	452	4	16	409	4
8	554	5	17	435	4
9	420	4	18	354	4
OUT	3,488	35	IN	3,537	36
			TOTAL	7,025	71

The par-4 15th at Inverness: Some of the greatest architects of all time have combined to produce this shotmaker's paradise.

determine a victor. Billy Burke and George Elm were tied after 72 holes and headed out for the prescribed 36-hole playoff which was standard at the time. Unfortunately, they remained deadlocked after those two rounds. So out they went again for another 36-hole battle in which Burke vanquished Elm by a single shot. This survival test persuaded the United States Golf Association to revamp the playoff structure to 18 holes; sudden death if tied after that.

Inverness also hosted the 1957 Open, won by Dick Mayer in a playoff over Cary Middlecoff. This was also the first Open appearance by Jack Nicklaus. The course Mayer won on had been lengthened to almost 7,000 yards, and the number of bunkers was well on its way to the 110 it boasts today.

The next U.S. Open held at Inverness was preceded by the 1973 U.S. Amateur which heralded the emergence of Craig Stadler, who would remain a force on the professional scene for the next 25 years. But in 1979, the Open returned, eventually making Hale Irwin a two-time winner of the national

championship. Although Irwin made it interesting by playing well in the middle rounds and then staggering in with a double-bogey, bogey to win by only two shots, the real hero of the 1979 Open was a tree. Course renovations the previous year failed to take into account that players (notably Lon Hinkle) could now drive through a gap in the trees on the par-5 eighth hole onto the 17th fairway and make the hole ridiculously short. The night after the first round, the USGA arranged for a 25-foot tree to be planted in the gap.

The 1979 Open was followed by the 1986 and 1993 PGA Championships. The 1986 event was notable because it marked another chapter in the miserable history of Greg Norman in major championships. With nine holes to play, Bob Tway trailed Norman by four shots. By the time they reached the 18th tee, they were even. Tway's approach caught the front right bunker while Norman typically spun his sand wedge off the green onto the fringe. Tway then holed his bunker shot for birdie while Norman missed his attempt.

Norman was also tied for the lead the next time the PGA came to Inverness. After four rounds, Norman and Paul Azinger had finished one shot ahead of Nick Faldo. Norman's putt lipped out on the first playoff hole and Azinger matched his par. On the second extra hole, Norman's putter let him down, and Azinger claimed the title.

The par-4 seventh is typical of Inverness, combining trees, water, and a treacherous putting surface.

———— Maui, Hawaii ————

KAPALUA

Golf Club

Architects: Ben Crenshaw, Bill Coore
Opened for Play: 1991

The 7,263-yard Plantation course completes the triple crown of superb golf experiences at Kapalua. (Mere mortals should play the regular tees at 6,547 yards!) The architects, Ben Crenshaw and Bill Coore, used this opportunity to put into practice their philosophy of applying traditional course architecture with modern environmental sensitivity. Working with the spectacular native topography provided the opportunity to showcase the grand scale of Kapalua with features such as massive bunkers, sweeping slopes, dramatic contouring, and panoramic views which may include the sight of whales cavorting in the strait below.

The par-4 first hole, aptly named "Kapalua," stretches 473 yards from the back tees. At 218 yards, the par-3 second hole favors a fade. The third hole, while suspiciously short for a par 4 on the

Plantation course, plays directly into the prevailing trade winds. It features a severely sloped and well-bunkered green. The fourth hole, "The High Road," is a traditional midlength par 4 which calls for a steady drive over a hill to a rolling fairway. The amoeba-shaped par-5 fifth hole favors the cut shot all the way to the green perched high on a peninsula above a canyon that borders the entire right side of the hole.

The spectacular sixth hole challenges course management skills with its alternate routes to the green: The courageous and skilled player will drive across the cliffs to the right side of the fairway. The faint of heart or less talented will go left, leaving a blind approach to the bowl-shaped green. The 484-yard, par-4 seventh hole plays much shorter than its yardage due to prevailing winds and its downward slope. A mid-iron across a canyon will hit the eighth hole's receptive green, a respite before attacking the par-5 ninth, perhaps the most demanding hole on the Plantation course. At 521 yards, the ninth demands three quality shots directly into the wind in order to reach the green. The tee shot must be solidly played into the fairway to allow the second to carry a large valley which rips across the hole about 260 yards short of the green. Shots failing to carry the valley leave blind approaches; those carrying the valley present a short-iron opportunity for a possible birdie. Realistically, par is a victory here.

The back nine commences with a short par 4 which, like the third hole, plays directly into the wind. Number 11 is the last par 3 at the Plantation course. The prevailing winds turn the 12th into a drive-and-pitch par 4, in contrast to the par-4 13th where the winds make all 407 yards a battle. After getting to the green with a low, wind-cheating drive and long-iron approach, much work remains. The putting surface is large, treacherously sloped, and that accursed wind even affects putts! At only 305 yards, 14 appears to be a sure birdie chance. But the ever-present winds will test any attempt to stick a ball close on this tiny green sitting atop a plateau.

"Switchback," the 555-yard, par-5 15th hole, is a double dogleg featuring strong slopes, crossing winds, and another canyon

Kapalua's Village course, adjacent to the Plantation course, climbs to 800 feet above sea level, mingling with pines, pineapple fields, and a lake.

KAPALUA GOLF CLUB
MAUI, HAWAII

HOLE	YARDAGE	PAR
1	473	4
2	218	3
3	380	4
4	382	4
5	532	5
6	398	4
7	484	4
8	203	3
9	521	5
OUT	3,591	36
10	354	4
11	164	3
12	373	4
13	407	4
14	305	4
15	555	5
16	365	4
17	486	4
18	663	5
IN	3,672	37
TOTAL	7,263	73

TEES	LENGTH	PAR	RATING
CHAMPIONSHIP	7,263	73	75.2
REGULAR	6,547	73	71.9
FRONT	5,627	75	73.2

that borders the teeing ground as well as the green. Flirting with this natural disaster will afford the nervy player a better chance at birdie. The 16th is a strategist's delight: A string of fairway bunkers on a diagonal from left to right strongly influences tee shot decisions. Drives played powerfully and accurately over those bunkers afford the best angle of attack to all pins except those set far left. Although indecently long at 486 yards,

the par-4 17th is reasonably reachable because of the assisting winds and a downhill slope exceeding 150 feet from tee to green. A long running draw is the best tee shot; even so, the approach still requires a long-iron or fairway wood.

Your round at the Plantation course concludes on the hole around which the rest of the course was formulated — a 663-yard downhill, downwind par 5. Believe it or not, the hole is reachable with two powerful blows assisted by slope and wind. The large, receptive fairway and green are difficult to judge owing to the vast panoramas and scale of the background.

The Plantation course is home to the annual Lincoln-Mercury Kapalua International, a nationally televised PGA Tour-affiliated event, which was formerly played at the Bay course. The Bay course offers relaxed play in tropical surroundings. Under azure blue skies, the course rolls out to the sea's edge where the sapphire Pacific and Neighbor Islands stretch out in front of you. Sailing ships frequent the sheltered waters, and in winter, giant humpback whales spout and frolic offshore. Palm trees, ironwoods, and stately Cook pines line the lush green fairways.

The Village course, adjacent to the Plantation course, is a challenging 18-hole layout that climbs from the foot of the West Maui mountains to 800 feet above sea level to mingle with pineapple fields, Cook pines, and a shimmering lake. The breathtaking scenery and panoramic views serve as a constant distraction from hitting the pure shots the layout requires.

The eighth hole at Kapalas's Plantation course requires an accurate mid- or long-iron tee shot over a ravine to a receptive green. But beware the treacherous trade winds!

— Hilton Head Island, South Carolina —

LONG COVE

Club

Architect: Pete Dye
Opened for Play: 1982

In *The Architects of Golf,* the point-form summary of Pete Dye's career consumes more than a page, one of the longest such biographies in that scholarly tome. According to authors Geoffrey Cornish and Ron Whitten, "Dye had done a series of low-budget courses in the Midwest by 1963, when he and [wife] Alice toured the great courses of Scotland. When they returned, Pete began to incorporate into his designs several of the principles they had observed in Scotland, including small greens, undulating fairways, pot bunkers, railroad tie bulkheads, and deep native roughs."

In the intervening decades, Dye has created a school of course design that has been criticized for being "too much" — Scotland on steroids, St. Andrews on acid. Pot bunkers like Florida sinkholes, railroad tie bulkheads resembling log cabins, incessantly undulating

fairways that require cart drivers to ingest anti-nausea medication. But for every PGA West and every TPC at Sawgrass, there has been an Honors in Tennessee, a Harbour Town Golf Links (also on Hilton Head Island), and others.

First among Dye's equals may be Long Cove, nestled in the heart of South Carolina's Hilton Head Island and built some 20 years after that fateful trip to the home of golf. Ask the architect's opinion and he'll just shrug his shoulders. "People always ask me how one of my courses ranks over another," he told *Links* magazine. "It's like ranking your kids. One is not necessarily better than the other, because they're all different." However, for traditionalists, Long Cove is definitely the favorite son. The fortunate residents of this development are generally of an earlier generation, one which enjoyed golf for golf's sake, and Dye kept that in mind when building the course.

The members can play from four sets of tees: 6,900 yards from the gold blocks, 6,420 from the blue, 5,873 from the white, and 5,002 from the red. While visually the course is intriguing, even imposing — there is water on a dozen holes and the sculptured bunkers seem to be everywhere — Dye has resisted the impulse to create situations which prevent higher handicappers from enjoying a round at Long Cove. "There's a lot of excitement there for the good player, but it's never unfair," Senior PGA Tour player Jim Ferree, who was the first director of golf here, told *Links*. "You won't have to hit the perfect golf shot to play the course. I think people like it so well because it's a fair test. And from an aesthetic standpoint, I believe it's one of the most beautiful courses in the world."

Ferree may be no more impartial than architect, author, and critic Tom Doak, who picks no less than four of the holes here (Nos. 1, 3, 5, and 11) as selections for Dye's all-time best 18 in his recent book, *The Confidential Guide to Golf Courses.* (Doak worked on the construction crew here when he was starting out in the business.) But their opinions stand up to scrutiny, because they are echoed by not only everyone who plays

here, but also the astute panelists from national golf magazines who rank Long Cove among the finest courses in America.

The first hole at Long Cove is an even 400 yards from the golds. A serpentine waste bunker writhes its way along the entire right-hand side of this hole, creating a whisper of hope for any ball headed even farther right into the water. The second hole is a great par 3 of almost 200 yards which offers a spectacular carry over water. The par-5 third hole is the No. 1 handicap hole with an ever-narrowing fairway with water defining its left periphery. As with most Dye courses, getting to the green does not necessarily merit a sigh of relief: Despite the rolling surfaces, multiple pin positions are possible, thus confounding even the members, not to mention their guests. The fourth is a straightforward par 4 with — surprise! — no water, while the fifth

TEES	LENGTH	PAR	RATING
GOLD	6,900	71	74.3
BLUE	6,420	71	71.9
WHITE	5,873	71	69.9
RED	5,002	71	69.5

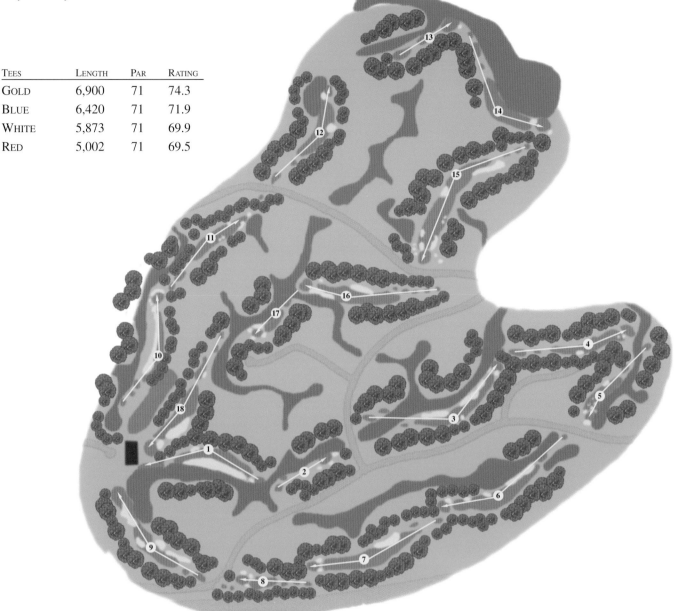

LONG COVE CLUB
HILTON HEAD ISLAND, SOUTH CAROLINA

HOLE	YARDAGE	PAR		HOLE	YARDAGE	PAR
1	400	4		10	403	4
2	196	3		11	376	4
3	539	5		12	445	4
4	384	4		13	137	3
5	317	4		14	410	4
6	513	5		15	590	5
7	439	4		16	460	4
8	203	3		17	210	3
9	428	4		18	450	4
OUT	3,419	36		IN	3,481	35
				TOTAL	6,900	71

is one of Dye's diabolical mini-par 4s. At only 317 from the tips, this hole requires self-control and precision to avoid the water, trees, and smattering of pot bunkers in front of the green. The sixth is another par 5 but, at 513 yards, is reachable with two sensible shots.

The sixth signals a three-hole stretch that Dye routed through an old dump site. These results must have reminded him of that long-ago trip to Scotland, for there is a definite links-style approach to this trio. The seventh dips and dives on its way to a sizable green

Number 15 is a tough par 5: Almost 600 yards long, it features both fairway and greenside bunkers.

protected by grassy hollows and a massive bunker. The par-3 eighth threatens errant shots with an epidemic of swales, hollows, and sand. The front nine concludes with an exercise in target golf, a par 4 that punctuates the tee, fairway, and green with spaghetti-strand waste bunkers.

The 10th hole is a mirror image of No. 1, with the water running down the left on this one. Number 11 is a great par 4. Well short of 400 yards in length, it demands accuracy, especially on the approach to the teardrop green. After the par-4 12th, the mischievously short 13th baffles even the most experienced player. Club selection is almost impossible when the wind is up. Many aficionados of hole design admire the 410-yard 14th, with its marshy mayhem lurking on the left from tee to green. Number 15 is a strong par 5 which tests the player's distance and accuracy; its 590-yard length is characterized by trees and expansive bunkers. The fairway of the par-4 16th snakes between two long fairway bunkers before ending at a diamond-shaped green, and the par-3 17th threatens every tee shot with more water, trees, and a

green girdled by four hungry bunkers. By the time you hit your tee shot on the dogleg-right 18th, you will agree with Pete Dye: "Long Cove is a nice piece of property. It lends itself to a timeless design."

The 410-yard 14th at Long Cove provokes much comment about the marshy wasteland which stretches from tee to green.

Hawaii, Hawaii

MAUNA KEA

Resort

Architect: Robert Trent Jones
Opened for Play: 1964

The original Mauna Kea is the mountain which dominates the Big Island of Hawaii. The other Mauna Kea is the golf course which, many attest, dominates the game on the island, thanks to the efforts of Laurance Rockefeller and Robert Trent Jones. Hawaii became a state in 1959, and local authorities invited Rockefeller to assist them in finding a way to lessen the tourist burden on Waikiki.

Rockefeller scouted sites around the island, locating a parcel wedged between the mountain and Kauna'oa Bay. Not only was there a gorgeous white sand beach for winter-weary travelers, there were also 230 acres that could be transformed into a golf course — if only the property wasn't buried in black lava. Rockefeller knew just the man to solve this dilemma. Bringing in Robert Trent Jones, then approaching the pinnacle of a stellar career, was a stroke of

genius. Jones surveyed the property and did a masterful routing for a site that had no soil. The solution? Grind up the 5,000-year-old lava, cover it with crushed coral, coat that with a layer of fertilizer, and then seed it. The success of this radical thought process is self-evident today as this verdant gem overlooking the azure Pacific sweeps over the countryside, through lava outcrops and exotic native vegetation.

Both Rockefeller and Jones must have been proud of the widespread acclaim which greeted and continues to greet their prodigy. Mauna Kea continues to garner top 100 rankings from *Golf Digest*, which also named it the top course in the state. *Golf* magazine has bestowed its vaunted Golf Medal on the resort, and *Meetings and Conventions* magazine awarded Mauna Kea a Gold Tee Award in 1995. The Mauna Kea Beach Hotel, managed by Prince Resorts Hawaii, reopened after a complete restoration in 1996. Prince Resorts Hawaii also operates the Hapuna Beach Price Hotel, the Maui Prince Hotel, and the Hawaii Prince Hotel-Waikiki, offering a total

of 99 holes of championship golf on three Hawaiian islands. The Hapuna course is an Arnold Palmer-Ed Seay design which nestles into the dramatic natural contours of the land right from the shoreline to about 700 feet above sea level. This sister course to Mauna Kea also offers spectacular views of the Kohala coast and the Pacific Ocean under the mountain's watchful eye.

Jones's basic design philosophy has been turned into one of golf's biggest clichés: "Every hole should be a difficult par but an easy bogey," or something to that effect. The trouble is that, in many cases, his courses reflect that slogan accurately. Mauna Kea is no exception. The fairways are generous, the bunkers are intended to indicate the line of play rather than engulf an errant shot...just another day in Paradise until you stand over your approach shot. For it is then that you appreciate Jones's master plan. Many of the approaches are uphill to well-bunkered, elevated, and severe greens on which the surrounding ocean, mountains, and winds make reading a putt extremely difficult. The entire

At almost 250 yards from the back tees, the 11th hole forces the player to use the appropriate tee deck.

Scenic But Sinister

The third hole is widely recognized as Mauna Kea's signature hole. From the back tees, this par 3 plays 210 yards over the surging surf of the Pacific to a green dangling from the side of the island. Towering palms stand sentinel, observing the often futile efforts of awestruck high-handicappers to reach the putting surface.

course features dramatic elevation changes, dogleg holes, and a total of 120 bunkers, many more than the average layout.

Noteworthy holes include the 11th, a par 3 which stretches 247 yards from tee to green. Take the pro's advice before starting out and play the tees appropriate for your ability, otherwise you will remember this hole as a short but difficult par 4! The par-4 14th is a challenging dogleg left while No. 17, a 555-yard par 5, will dare the big hitter to get home in two. And the tees on the finishing holes on both nines rise to an elevation of 200 feet, commanding a panoramic view of the ocean and the adjacent Mauna Kea resort.

Mauna Kea has played host to its share of prestigious events, beginning with a match between Jack Nicklaus, Arnold Palmer, and Gary Player to publicize its opening in 1964. Nicklaus and Palmer tied after four rounds at 13-under 275 while Player was three shots back. That 275 total remains the course's 72-hole record while Jack and Arnie share the nine-hole record of 31 set during the same match. In 1968, Shell's Wonderful World of Golf, hosted by the legendary Jimmy Demaret, pitted Al Geiberger against Dan Sikes and Peter Allis. Geiberger prevailed with a solid 69 to Sikes's 71 and Allis's 72. Qualifying rounds have been held here for PGA events and the U.S. Open.

MAUNA KEA RESORT
HAWAII, HAWAII

HOLE	YARDAGE	PAR
1	383	4
2	394	4
3	210	3
4	413	4
5	593	5
6	344	4
7	204	3
8	530	5
9	427	4
OUT	3,498	36
10	554	5
11	247	3
12	387	4
13	409	4
14	413	4
15	201	3
16	422	4
17	555	5
18	428	4
IN	3,616	36
TOTAL	7,114	72

TEES	LENGTH	PAR	RATING
BLACK	7,114	72	73.6
BLUE	6,737	72	71.9
ORANGE	6,365	72	70.1
WHITE	5,277	72	65.2

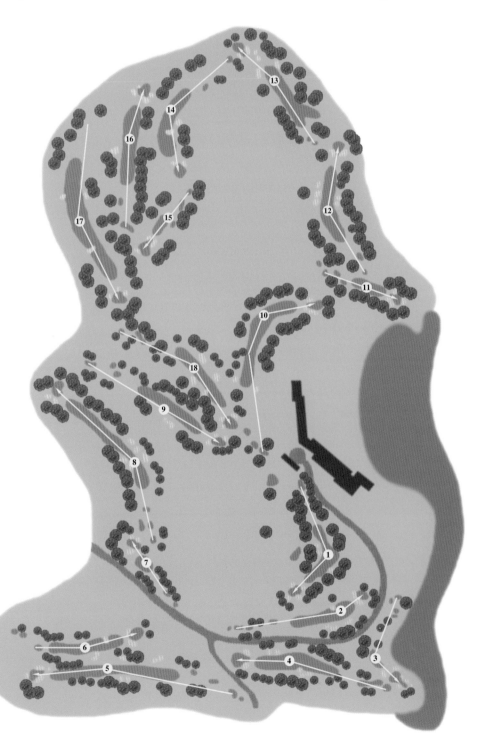

An extra club is recommended when hitting onto the elevated green of the par-5 10th hole.

The sixth hole is another green which requires one, maybe two, extra clubs.

Merion's 11th hole is a classic short par 4 with a green encircled by water. It was here that Bobby Jones completed the Grand Slam in 1930.

——— *Ardmore, Pennsylvania* ———

MERION

Golf Club

Architect: Hugh Wilson
Opened for Play: 1912

When golfers speak reverently of "Merion," it is the East course to which they refer. Opened for play in 1912, both the East and West layouts were the work of Hugh Wilson, a prominent amateur of the time but a neophyte designer. Two years earlier, he called upon famed architect Charles Blair Macdonald at the site of his National Golf Links of America in New York State. Macdonald recommended Wilson visit the British Isles and absorb some of the timeless lessons offered by the ancient links of Scotland, Ireland, and England. Judging from the result — famed golf writer Herbert Warren Wind called it "America's classic course" — Wilson was a stellar student.

Merion's roots date back to 1896 when the Golf Committee of the Merion Cricket Club recommended building nine holes on rented

What the par-3 13th lacks in length, it more than makes up in treachery. Missing its bowl-shaped green almost always leads to a bogey.

Although the par-3 ninth hole has two tee pads, neither avoids carrying the creek, pond, and bunkers which protect the boldly contoured green.

land. Nine more opened for play in 1900, and this rudimentary 18, the Haverford course, satisfied the rapidly growing membership until the advent of the Haskell ball made such truncated layouts obsolete. (The Haskell, with its wound rubber core, far outdistanced its predecessor, the gutta-percha.) A more appropriate site was procured, Wilson was enlisted, and the rest is golf history.

Many golfers, unfamiliar with Merion itself, would nonetheless recognize one widely publicized trademark of the club: the wicker baskets which top each flagstick and grace the club's logo. As noted in the club's history, it was not until 1989 that a reasonable theory was put forth concerning the origin of this idiosyncrasy. After a visit to Merion, Tony Nickson, a British golf historian, sent the club a copy of a painting titled *First International Match, Scotland v. England, Prestwick Golf Club, 1903.* One figure in the painting was a young caddie, holding a flagstick topped with a wicker. No doubt course architect Hugh Wilson, in his travels abroad prior to designing Merion, noted this innovation. Aside from their curious appearance, the wickers do not indicate wind conditions to the player as a conventional flag would. In addition, the flagsticks themselves are eight feet tall, thus further confounding the golfer.

No less an advocate than Jack Nicklaus, who has said Merion is in his top five favorite courses in the world, argues that Merion can hold its own against the newcomers. "I love Merion," he said in the 1981 U.S. Open program. "It is one of those old-time golf courses that doesn't have the length of some of the modern-day courses, but it

Standing The Test Of Time

Although Merion's challenge as a modern championship course has been questioned because of its relatively short length (6,482 yards), its superlative design and tournament record belie those queries.

As Desmond Tolhurst notes in the club's fine history book: "It was at Merion that Chick Evans achieved his Double Crown in 1916, winning the U.S. Amateur after his U.S. Open victory earlier that year. It was at Merion that Bobby Jones completed his Grand Slam, winning the 1930 U.S. Amateur to go with victories in the U.S. Open and British Open and Amateur the same year. It was in the 1950 U.S. Open at Merion that Ben Hogan made his thrilling comeback from a near-fatal auto accident. Merion witnessed Jack Nicklaus's incredible 269 in the 1960 World Amateur and his later defeat at the hands of Lee Trevino in the 1971 U.S. Open. Trevino's victory at Merion was the first of an incredible Triple Crown where he won the U.S. Open, Canadian Open, and British Open in a period of 20 days. Merion also saw David Graham's grand come-from-behind effort in the final round of the 1981 U.S. Open, the first victory by an Australian in our national championship."

This unique commemorative trophy was commissioned to salute Lee Trevino's rare "Triple Crown."

still stands the test. That's the mark of a great golf course to me. You've really got to play golf to win at Merion." Several years after his World Amateur win, he remarked: "I think Merion is a perfect example of the principle that a golf course does not have to be long to be a great test of golf. The greens are beautifully designed with very subtle contours." Prior to the 1971 Open, Nicklaus, a prodigious driver of the ball at the time, chastised reporters who proposed to criticize the course because it put a premium on accuracy: "On a course where you can just lean back and belt one 300 yards off the tee, you don't need to think. Merion is a thinking man's course and I like it."

What Merion may lack in length, it more than makes up in subtlety, even deceit.

MERION GOLF CLUB
ARDMORE, PENNSYLVANIA

HOLE	YARDAGE	PAR		HOLE	YARDAGE	PAR
1	362	4		10	310	4
2	536	5		11	369	4
3	181	3		12	371	4
4	600	5		13	127	3
5	418	4		14	408	4
6	420	4		15	366	4
7	350	4		16	428	4
8	360	4		17	220	3
9	179	3		18	463	4
OUT	3,420	36		IN	3,062	34
				TOTAL	6,482	70

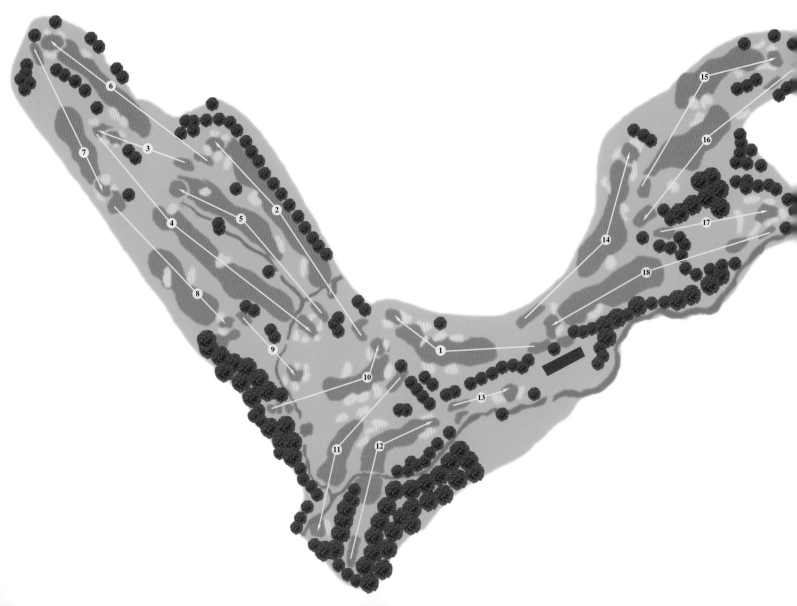

Nothing is as it appears, with swales, hollows, and "the White Faces of Merion" complicating every shot. (Chick Evans dubbed Merion's beautiful bunkers "the White Faces" on his way to winning the 1916 U.S. Amateur.)

Merion's two par 5s appear during the first six holes: The 536-yard second hole offers a landing area only 25 yards wide to compensate for its length, and the landing area of the 600-yard fourth hole slopes sharply left to right, severely penalizing the faded tee shot. The fifth hole is the top handicap hole, a 418-yard par 4 with a creek defining the entire left boundary. Holes seven through 13 average only about 300 yards, although they may present an insurmountable obstacle to achieving par.

The last three holes have been called the toughest three-hole stretch in the world. The 16th is the "Quarry Hole," a 428-yard par 4 which challenges the better player to carry a disused rock quarry to get to the green. The quarry again comes into play on 17, a 220-yard par 3 with a green encircled by bunkers. On the mighty 18th, a 463-yard par 4, Ben Hogan hit a 1-iron onto the green on the 72nd hole of the 1950 U.S. Open. The resulting par tied him for the lead. He won the playoff the next day despite the fact that his 1-iron was stolen from his bag prior to the round.

Approach shots on the par-4 16th hole must carry a disused quarry filled with sand, brush, and other unpleasantness.

The fifth hole at Muirfield Village has it all.
This dogleg-right par 5 demands accuracy and
length to avoid the trees, water, and bunkers.

———— Dublin, Ohio ————

MUIRFIELD VILLAGE

Architects: Jack Nicklaus, Desmond Muirhead
Opened for Play: 1974

It's almost unfair that the man who is the greatest professional golfer of all time should be able to design a golf course that is among the best in the world. Even though Jack Nicklaus had the able assistance of Desmond Muirhead, the Salvador Dali of golf architecture, he managed to put his own stamp on this tremendous property a few miles outside of Columbus, Ohio.

Muirfield Village was the culmination of a dream for Nicklaus, who wanted to create a great golf facility combining the finest aspects of all the courses he had admired, including the original Muirfield in Scotland where he won his first British Open. The astute visitor to Muirfield Village can recognize design features from some very famous courses around the world. A major clue comes at the par-3 12th hole which closely resembles its counterpart at Augusta National.

Nicklaus had two primary objectives when designing and building his course. The first was to create a tough but fair challenge, not only for the professionals who would visit there every May during the PGA Tour's Memorial Tournament, but also for the members. His philosophy is that golf should be at least as much a game of precision as of power; that observing, thinking, and planning should be as much required of a player as skill and strength; and that golf should be played in beautiful surroundings. The second objective was perhaps unique at the time in golf history: Nicklaus sought to provide the best possible facilities for spectators. As a result, Muirfield Village, with its spectator mounds and amphitheater effects around the greens, is known as one of the best places in the world for watching a tournament.

It is also one of the best places in the world to play in a tournament, say the touring professionals who have heaped praise on the course since the day it opened. By 1977, just three years after its birth and one year after the first Memorial Tournament, *Golf Digest* ranked it among the top 20 courses in the

MUIRFIELD VILLAGE
DUBLIN, OHIO

HOLE	YARDAGE	PAR		HOLE	YARDAGE	PAR
1	446	4		10	441	4
2	452	4		11	538	5
3	392	4		12	156	3
4	204	3		13	442	4
5	531	5		14	363	4
6	430	4		15	490	5
7	549	5		16	204	3
8	189	3		17	430	4
9	410	4		18	437	4
OUT	3,603	36		IN	3,501	36
				TOTAL	7,104	72

TEES	LENGTH	PAR	RATING
MEMORIAL	7,104	72	75.8
BLUE	6,468	72	73.3
WHITE	6,210	72	71.1

country. The Tour pros have also named the course the best conditioned on Tour. The 1987 Ryder Cup brought Muirfield Village front and center on the world golfing stage when the European team upset the heavily favored Americans despite a valiant final effort by the U.S. squad in the singles matches.

The 446-yard, par-4 first hole is a slight dogleg right where your elevated tee shot lands on a wide fairway sloping from right to left. Bunkers in the landing area will catch the sliced or pushed drive; a hook or pull might find the creek threading through the woods that line the left side of the hole. The green is the largest on the course, although it is guarded by four bunkers. A creek flanks the entire right side of the 452-yard, par-4

second hole from about 100 yards out and abuts the right edge and area of the green. Trees impede the approach of a drive hit too far left, and the green is bunkered front right and rear left. Thus, the player must drive and approach toward water, and accuracy is at a premium. The third hole is the No. 1 stroke hole. At less than 400 yards, length is not the issue. A downhill drive to a generous fairway is followed by an approach over a lake to a small, two-tiered green cut into a hillside. A drive too far left might find a creek at the woodline, leaving nowhere to drop out that permits a clear shot to the green. Water awaits a weak approach, and sand will claim the foolhardy soul who overshoots the mark.

The fourth hole is the first of Muirfield

"We Won The Cup!"

During the last week of September in 1987, a team of European golfers triumphed over the U.S. squad in the 27th Ryder Cup matches, the first time the Europeans had ever won on American soil. It was indisputable proof that the top Europeans were at least a match for the best the Americans had to offer. The first day featured foursomes in the morning (U.S. 2, Europe 2) with four-ball matches in the afternoon (U.S. 0, Europe 4). The formats were reversed the following day, but the outcome was not, with the U.S. trailing 10 ½ to 5 ½, entering the third and final day. Although the home team played desperately for at least a tie, meaning the trophy would remain here, the visitors held on to register a stunning 15-13 win. A throng of European supporters hoisted diminutive Ian Woosnam to their shoulders and paraded around Muirfield Village, chanting, "We won the Cup! We won the Cup!"

Village's four par 3s and, at 204 yards, presents a real challenge. It slopes gently downhill to a long, narrow, heavily trapped green cut into a hillside. Disaster lurks in a wooded depression left of the green. The par-5 fifth hole presents another downhill tee shot between wooded hillsides to a wide, level fairway. Then the fun starts. Some 300 yards out, a creek bordering the left side of the hole swings into the fairway which it then bisects all the way to the green. On No. 6, an oak tree over the lake fronting the green blocks the approach from a drive hit too far right, but a cluster of bunkers cut into the hillside is equally threatening to the left.

At 549 yards from the back tees, the seventh hole is reachable by only the longest hitters. "An exposed, elevated, bunker-lined, double-doglegged hole" is how the course guide describes it. The par-3 eighth hole returns you to wooded country, this time dogwood, beech, and hickory. Number nine tests your nerve with a tee shot that cannot stray too far right (trees block your approach) or too far left (a

The par-4 third hole is the No. 1 stroke hole and perhaps No. 1 in the scenery department, too.

A creek guards the right-hand side of the second fairway, making this par 4 one of the toughest at Muirfield Village.

steep wooded hillside lurks to gobble your ball). The tilted green is spectacularly framed by a lake, a creek, a forest, and a hillside.

Sand guards both sides of the landing area on 10, and a large, tentacled bunker fronts the green on this 441-yard par 4. The par-5 11th hole is a prototypical spectator hole which runs the length of a valley between high, wooded hills. The hole looks deceptively easy, but watch out for the creek which cuts across the fairway 320 yards out. The 12th is a photographer's delight: The tee shot is played from a wooded hillside across water to a kidney-shaped green cut into another hillside.

On 13, the ideal tee shot out of the wooded chute will find the right half of the fairway for the best angle into the long, narrow green. At only 363 yards, the 14th features a creek which angles across the fairway some 245 yards out. The 15th, a short par 5, is arrowstraight through the forest, rewarding accuracy rather than length.

Number 16 is a powerful par 3 at 204 yards from the back tees and sets the tone for the 17th, a demanding par 4 with a bunker the size of a football field encroaching into the landing area. As you come up 18, the spectacular par-4 finishing hole, try to imagine the scene when 20,000 spectators surround the green during the Memorial Tournament.

The Memorial is based on a unique concept. Each year, the Captain's Club, a distinguished group of golfing statesmen who advise on the format and conduct of the event, selects one person, living or dead, who has played golf with conspicuous honor. The Memorial is in recognition of their life and achievements. Honorees have included Bobby Jones, Walter Hagen, Sam Snead, Old Tom Morris and Young Tom Morris, Byron Nelson, and Glenna Collett Vare.

*The sixth hole at Oak Hill is unique because it is
the only hole that is not part of the original
Donald Ross design. In 1976, architects George and
Tom Fazio designed this outstanding par 3.*

——————— *Rochester, New York* ———————

OAK HILL

Country Club

*Architect: Donald Ross
Opened for Play: 1926*

Playing Oak Hill's East course today, it is almost impossible to believe that this site was described as "barren, cheerless, and singularly lacking in beauty" in the 1920s. That was when the University of Rochester swapped these 355 acres with the nine-hole Oak Hill Club, which had a more attractive though smaller property on the Genesee River. Not a bad deal: In addition to the land, the university would foot the bill for two 18-hole courses and a clubhouse.

The shrewd club members made the best of the deal by constructing a sprawling classic Tudor-style clubhouse filled with gorgeous woodwork and by contracting Donald Ross, the genius from Pinehurst, to design the 36-hole complex. Ross, undeterred by the less than generous remarks directed at the raw piece of ground, persuaded Oak Hill's members that the site potentially could possess

The 13th green sits in a natural spectator setting. It is also surrounded by the "Hill of Fame" — a collection of oak trees, each of which is dedicated to individuals who have made an outstanding contribution to golf.

"remarkable beauty" and could become "one of the finest golf courses in the United States." The results proved that this was more than mere salesmanship on the part of Ross.

"Bunkers were dished out of hillsides and cut in the face of slopes, knolls, and terraces," says one of the club's historical publications authored by Donald Kladstrup. Ross "leveled some ridges, because he wanted visible greens, greens that could be seen from the tees. The course of Allen's Creek also was altered in several places, including a widening to create small ponds on Holes 11 and 13 of the East Eighteen. Overall, however, Ross sought to adapt the terrain without major

changes…It is the East course, however, that has received the most attention. At least partly because of the interesting water hazards posed by Allen's Creek, it has been host to a number of major tournaments. Each of these events, for various reasons, has in turn precipitated new efforts to refine and toughen the existing layout."

The meandering creek, the rolling topography, and the surrounding woods did give the site some potential. Adding Ross's supreme ability gave it a fighting chance to become a great course. The final ingredient was the dedication and love lavished upon the club and its courses by generations of members, notably Dr. John R. Williams. Led by Williams, a self-taught arborist, Oak Hill has been transformed from that "barren" site to its present-day glamour through the planting and nurturing of more than 75,000 trees.

Oak Hill's love affair with high-level tournaments began in 1934. Coincidentally, that year marked Rochester's centennial and the 20th anniversary of native son Walter Hagen's first U.S. Open win. Thus, the Hagen Centennial Open was held and won by Leo Diegel, who ironically had ended Hagen's string of four consecutive PGA Championships six years earlier. In 1941, a local newspaper put up a $5,000 purse, an amount significant enough to attract a field with the likes of Ben Hogan, Sam Snead, Lloyd Mangrum, and Jug McSpaden. Snead blew Hogan and the rest away by seven shots, although Hogan ran away with the 1942 version.

In 1949, the U.S. Amateur was held at Oak Hill, a year after USGA executive director Joe Dey came to assess the course. "Where have you been for 20 years?" he asked incredulously. "There's nothing like this in the whole country!" Seven years later, the USGA brought its major tournament to Rochester; that Open was claimed by Cary Middlecoff with a one-over-par total of 281. In a weak moment that would come back to haunt him, Hogan had this comment during a practice round prior to the championship: "This is the easiest golf course I've ever seen for a U.S. Open." Hogan finished at two over par, in a tie for second with Julius Boros.

The Open returned in 1968 when Lee Trevino hit the scene like a Texas whirlwind, becoming the first golfer in history to shoot

The Challenge

The No. 1 stroke hole at Oak Hill is the very first hole faced by a player: The Challenge. Ben Hogan has called it the toughest starting hole in golf and for good reason, says club historian Donald Kladstrup. "On three separate occasions, in 1941, 1942, and 1946, he took a six. In the 1956 U.S. Open, when he was seeking an all-time record fifth Open title, he took a five here on his final round that saw him lose the tournament by one stroke to Dr. Cary Middlecoff. With lots of trees and a threatening bunker on the left, The Challenge must be played as a dogleg. Driving the ball too far to the right flirts with a possible out-of-bounds penalty. A good drive still leaves significant yardage to be negotiated. Complicating matters further is Allen's Creek, which crosses the fairway 80 yards in front of a green jealously guarded by three hungry bunkers."

Oak Hill Country Club
Rochester, New York

HOLE	YARDAGE	PAR
1	440	4
2	401	4
3	211	3
4	570	5
5	406	4
6	167	3
7	431	4
8	430	4
9	419	4
OUT	3,475	35
10	432	4
11	192	3
12	372	4
13	594	5
14	323	4
15	177	3
16	439	4
17	458	5
18	440	4
IN	3,427	36
TOTAL	6,902	71

TEES	LENGTH	PAR	RATING
BLUE	6,902	71	73.8
WHITE	6,519	71	72.3
RED	5,866	75	74.4

Perched on the highest point of Oak Hill, the par-3 15th hole features a sloped green bracketed by bunkers and a pond.

The genius of Donald Ross is evident on the third hole at Oak Hill. Nothing less than a perfect tee shot will guarantee par.

four rounds in the 60s in a U.S. Open. Between Trevino's milestone and the next major championship at Oak Hill, the 1980 PGA won by Jack Nicklaus, the club decided major renovations were required to provide the course with more weapons to defend against the pros. George and Tom Fazio were brought in, with results which generated controversy. The negative comments centered around the fact that Oak Hill now had 14 holes designed by Ross and four by the Fazios.

The 1984 Senior Open, won by Miller Barber, was the next visitor, followed by the 1989 U.S. Open which made Curtis Strange the first back-to-back Open winner since Hogan in 1950 and 1951. Another unique feature of the '89 Open was when four players — Doug Weaver, Mark Wiebe, Jerry Pate, and Nick Price — all aced the sixth hole within two hours.

But it isn't a long shot that Oak Hill, which hosted the 1995 Ryder Cup Matches (won by Europe 14 ½ to 13 ½) and will be the site of the 1998 U.S. Amateur, will continue to figure prominently in the hearts of golfers, pro and amateur, for many years to come.

Renowned architect Donald Ross designed both the North and South courses at Michigan's Oakland Hills. However, the South course is known around the golfing world as "The Monster." Here is the par-4 11th.

———— Birmingham, Michigan ————

OAKLAND HILLS

Country Club

Architect: Donald Ross
Opened for Play: 1918

The Monster. Ben Hogan bestowed that label on Oakland Hills Country Club's South course after winning the 1951 U.S. Open. "I'm just glad that I brought this course, this monster, to its knees," he gasped after registering what many still feel was the finest round of tournament golf ever. His final-round 67 stunned many observers, primarily Robert Trent Jones who had concocted the most punitive test ever presented to the world's finest golfers, "the world's most severe test of golf."

One player snarled that the fairway landing areas were so narrow that players had to walk down them single file. In reality, they were about 25 yards wide; missing them meant first trying to find the ball in the shin-deep rough and then attempting to advance it toward the green. Supported by the club's directors, Jones had set out a year

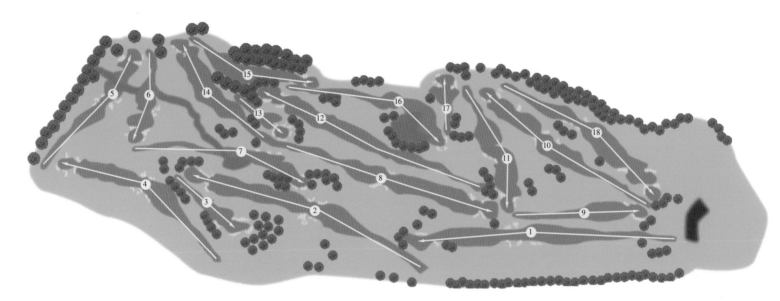

OAKLAND HILLS COUNTRY CLUB
BIRMINGHAM, MICHIGAN
SOUTH COURSE

HOLE	YARDAGE	PAR			
1	434	4	10	455	4
2	528	5	11	431	4
3	199	3	12	556	5
4	437	4	13	171	3
5	465	4	14	480	4
6	360	4	15	396	4
7	405	4	16	409	4
8	482	5	17	202	3
9	218	3	18	480	5
OUT	3,528	36	IN	3,580	36
			TOTAL	7,108	72

before with one clear mandate: to make the course the toughest any player had ever encountered. When a player reached into his bag, Jones wanted any club to come out except for the driver, "that yard-consuming club which more than any other has made a mockery of par." Aside from Hogan's machinelike precision, Jones had achieved his goal. No player broke par during the first round; the scoring average was 78.4. Indeed, the terrifying 14th hole did not surrender a single birdie to any competitor during the 1951 Open.

In envisioning his redesign, Jones's mental image was "double-target golf," meaning that the player would be challenged to find a precise target area off the tee and another upon his approach to the green. The player bold or foolhardy enough to hit driver and unlucky enough to miss the landing area in these hourglass-shaped fairways would be hitting his next shot from some unpleasant country. During his extensive renovation, Jones had filled in bunkers and moved them farther down the fairway to reflect the modern player's ability to hit the ball longer due to technological advances in ball and club manufacture. Their presence about 250 yards from the tee meant a ball even slightly off line would be swallowed, although that was the preferred option over Oakland Hills' rough and trees. The dogleg-left 15th hole even features a crossbunker in the heart of the fairway.

Certainly, back in 1917, Donald Ross never anticipated that the course he laid out would revolutionize tournament golf (and not necessarily for the better). Ross, the world's premier golf architect, was invited by the Board of Oakland Hills to lay out a top-notch members' course on 400 acres of rolling farmland near Detroit. Not content with the top architect, the Board also acquired the services of Walter Hagen, one of the top players anywhere, as their first professional. Although Hagen, the 1914 U.S. Open champion, stayed but one year, the refusal of those founding members to accept anything less than the best was to remain a hallmark of Oakland Hills.

While Ross would also design the club's North course, which opened in 1923 as a public facility, it is for the South 18 that Oakland Hills is internationally renowned. The routing, over some tremendously undulating topography, was superb. Few flat lies are discovered, even in the fairways. The greens, as Jones would report in his autobiography, were

incomparable: "Ross's great greens, with their crowns, swales, terraces, and slopes, were large enough and needed little revamping." That observation confirms Jones's brilliance for he was smart enough to respect the presence of genius. However, true to his punitive mandate, he did install bunkers around many of those "great greens" to further confound the poor golfer. In all, he added almost 70 bunkers to the South course in preparation for the Open.

From the start, Oakland Hills was intended to challenge both the members as well as the top amateurs and professionals. In order to measure its success, the club has been generous in playing host to premier events in both categories. The 1922 Western Open was the first championship played on the South course, although the club's hospitality

The 18th hole on the South course has provided a thrilling finish to many championships, including U.S. Opens and PGA Championships.

was slightly tainted — the event was won by Mike Brady, the host professional. The U.S. Open first arrived in 1924 when dark horse Cyril Walker of England nosed out Bobby Jones by three shots. The 1929 U.S. Women's Amateur preceded another U.S. Open in 1937, which would be won by Ralph Guldahl by two strokes over Sam Snead. Guldahl would successfully defend in 1938 while Snead would never win a U.S. Open.

Ten years after the storied 1951 championship, the Open returned and was claimed by Gene Littler. Bobby Nichols would win the Carling World Golf Championship in 1964. In the 1972 PGA Championship, Gary Player hit many fine shots on his way to the title, although one stands out: After pushing his tee shot on 16 into the rough behind the willow trees, he hammered a 9-iron over the trees to within three feet of the flagstick for a birdie. The PGA Championship returned in 1979 and was won by David Graham in a playoff over Ben

Crenshaw. Senior U.S. Opens arrived in 1981 (won by Arnold Palmer) and 1991 (won by Jack Nicklaus). Andy North won the 1985 U.S. Open which was perhaps more notorious for the fate of T. C. Chen. Chen was leading the tournament on Sunday when he double-hit a wedge shot on the fifth hole. The resulting quadruple-bogey eight led to a complete collapse, a second-place tie with Denis Watson and Dave Barr, and the nickname T. C. (Two Chip) Chen. The 1996 Open was won by Steve Jones.

In 1937, the course was lengthened to more than 7,000 yards in order to test that generation of players who now packed steel-shafted clubs, wound balls, and sand wedges. Then Jones wreaked his havoc in 1950. And now, yet again, the birthplace of target golf is threatened with being made obsolete by technology. Despite the creation of some new championship tees, the bunkers planted by Jones are now routinely flown by today's players. Is a new "monster" on the drawing board?

A "Player's" Course

The 16th hole on Oakland Hill's South course is regarded as a difficult hole by everyone who plays this intimidating par 4, with its green protected by water, bunkers, and trees. However, in the 1972 PGA Championship, Gary Player lofted a 9-iron from behind the willow trees to within three feet of the stick. The resulting birdie helped him win the title.

The par-4 fifth (left) and the par-5 12th (below) on the South course illustrate Oakland Hills' distinctive characteristics: spectacular trees, immaculate conditioning, and heavily contoured greens.

———— Oakmont, Pennsylvania ————

OAKMONT

Country Club

Architect: Henry Clay Fownes
Opened for Play: 1904

The course guide for Oakmont is elegant and understated — like all things at Oakmont. The guide's author calls the layout "a course that can be a nightmare." The guide continues: "Oakmont was designed and built by Henry Clay Fownes in 1903. He was an iron and steel tycoon who really knew how to get things done. The course was built in only a few months. Construction began on the morning of September 15, 1903, using 150 men and two dozen mule teams. Twelve holes were finished six weeks later when work was halted because of the winter, and the other six holes were completed the next spring. It was opened for play in the summer of 1904. Fownes pledged when he built the course that it would be the toughest layout in the world. The course has remained almost completely unchanged since it was laid out. Oakmont has undergone fewer alterations than any of the courses that host major championships.

"Henry C. Fownes was a very good golfer even though he started playing

when he was over 40 years old. Andrew Carnegie, a fellow steel magnate, introduced H. C. Fownes to the game of golf in 1899. Fownes qualified for the first of the four U.S. Amateur championships in which he competed in 1901. He retired from national competition in 1907. Fownes' son, William C. Fownes Jr., was his chief consultant. He was a very good golfer who qualified for the U.S. Amateur 25 times and won it at The Country Club in Brookline, Massachusetts, in 1910. He was the captain of the U.S. team in the first Walker Cup Matches in 1922 and served as the president of the United States Golf Association in 1926

and 1927. He became chairman of the Oakmont greens committee in 1911. William became the guardian of the course and continued the commitment to make Oakmont the toughest course in the world.

"The younger Fownes thought the course needed bunkers, so he directed the construction of traps around the green, along both sides of the fairway and even across some fairways. He would watch golfers play the course and whenever he saw a player hit over

OAKMONT COUNTRY CLUB
OAKMONT, PENNSYLVANIA

HOLE	YARDAGE	PAR			
1	467	4	10	462	4
2	346	4	11	382	4
3	425	4	12	602	5
4	564	5	13	185	3
5	382	4	14	360	4
6	199	3	15	471	4
7	435	4	16	232	3
8	253	3	17	319	4
9	478	5	18	456	4
OUT	3,549	36	IN	3,469	35
			TOTAL	7,018	71

TEES	LENGTH	PAR	RATING
CHAMPIONSHIP	7,018	71	75.5
MIDDLE	6,426	71	72.9
FORWARD	5,954	71	70.7

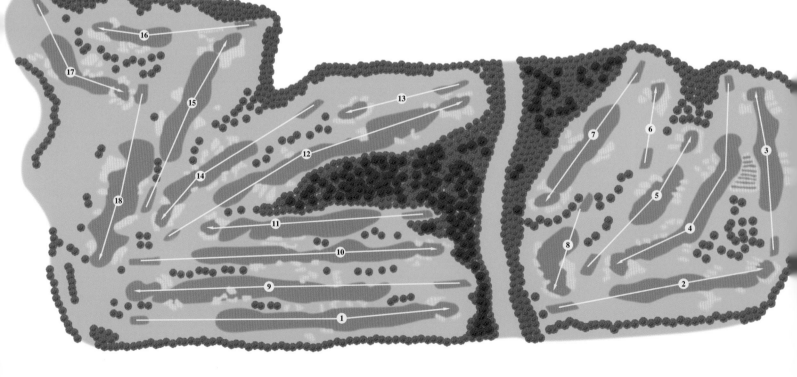

a fairway bunker or hit a poor shot that went unpunished, he would instruct the greenskeeper to excavate another bunker. At one time he had directed the installation of more than 350 bunkers. The Fownes' design philosophy was that 'a shot poorly played should be a shot irrevocably lost.'"

Oakmont is one of the most severely difficult courses in North America, featuring hard and slick greens, bunkers everywhere you look, narrow fairways bordered by thick rough, and more than adequate length. A penal design forces the player to follow the narrow route or flight lines laid out for him to hit from tee to green. Golfers are penalized severely if they make even minor errors. Oakmont is long and punishing.

Oakmont's greens are among the hardest and fastest in championship golf. They were built on a base of only six inches of topsoil over a foundation of clay. In the early days they were shaved as close as the mowing equipment could cut them, and then they were packed down by eight men pushing a 1,500-pound roller. These greens are frequently described as "scary," and everything possible is done to maintain their reputation.

In the 1953 U.S. Open, Ben Hogan hit a 6-iron close to the hole on the 18th. He made the putt to finish 3-3-3 and win by six shots over Sam Snead.

The 14th hole features a green 46 yards deep tucked behind several of the hole's 13 bunkers.

The third hole provides the player's first glimpse of the famed Church Pews bunker complex.

First Among Equals

Just imagine: the No. 1 stroke hole at what may be the most penal course in existence! And it's the very first hole at Oakmont, a 467-yard par 4 from the championship tees. Oakmont's course guide calls it "probably the toughest opening hole in the world" without much fear of contradiction. The tee shot has to hit the narrow landing area between the fairway bunkers. Trees and out of bounds threaten drives hit too far to the right. The approach shot is the most difficult at Oakmont: a blind downhill shot to a very undulating green that falls away from the golfer.

Each green has its unique characteristics for shot shapes due to individual configurations and undulations. It is not enough just to hit a green at Oakmont because there may be only one or two angles to the cup placement that allow you to really stroke the putt. Many of the greens slope front to back instead of the usual back to front. The members at Oakmont take pride in the fact that every green except one has remained where Henry Fownes put it. The eighth green had to be moved 10 yards in 1951 to make room for the Pennsylvania turnpike.

Oakmont's bunkers are certainly one of the main reasons that it is considered one of the world's toughest and most punishing courses. Nearly half of the 350 bunkers disappeared over the years, filled in after William Fownes relented under pressure from the members, but 180 remain, many of them golf landmarks. The "Church Pews" bunker between the third and fourth fairways is the famous hazard at Oakmont. It is a massive expanse of sand wasteland about the size of a football field, containing eight rows of grass that will catch pulled or hooked drives from either tee. A smaller copy of the Church Pews runs along the left side of the 15th fairway. In addition to the great length of the 253-yard eighth hole, this herculean par 3 is protected by the Sahara, a huge expanse of sand that is 130 yards long and 30 yards wide. The toughest bunker is the Big Mouth on the front right side of the green on the short uphill par-4 17th hole. The 18th hole is a 456-yard par 4 with lots of bunkers, especially the big crossbunker right in the middle of the fairway. There are many treacherous pot bunkers that are very deep and very strategically placed.

*The 18th at San Francisco's Olympic:
Only 347 yards long, it challenges
players with a tough tee shot followed
by a guarded green.*

——— *San Francisco, California* ———

OLYMPIC

Country Club

*Architect: Wilfrid Reid
Opened for Play: 1917*

Although San Francisco's exclusive Olympic Club owns a total of 54 golf holes, the Lakeside course is foremost here. Indeed, in 1987 this loop became the first course in the state to play host to three U.S. Opens. In contrast to the previous two, which were boisterous battles, the most recent Open produced a mild-mannered champion in Scott Simpson who outlasted Seve Ballesteros and Tom Watson.

The club deserves considerable credit for its foresight in purchasing a financially challenged course on the west side of the city shortly after World War I. By all accounts, the existing course was unremarkable: Built on sand hills a few hundred yards from the Pacific Ocean, it was notable only because the fairways were canted sideways at an almost unfair angle. There were almost no trees

The 433-yard ninth at Olympic is a long and narrow par 4.

and absolutely no water hazards. Today, there still are no water hazards, but the trees are another story. In fact, they are often said to be the only story at Lakeside.

Detractors say the arboreal overexuberance exhibited by management and members in the ensuing 75 years has created an extremely difficult course where the challenge is not presented by strength of individual holes or by the character of a great design. Lakeside's challenge, they contend, is in the almost impossible feat of avoiding the tens of thousands of trees which overhang tees,

greens, and fairways, creating a tunnel effect in places. One story, perhaps apocryphal in nature, recounts an instance where three branches were pruned from a single tree and more than 150 balls tumbled to the ground!

In addition to the trees and the heavy rough nurtured by San Francisco's moist climate, the tilted fairways reward only a left-to-right shot in most cases. Missing the fairway means sacrificing at least one shot to recover from the rough or the omnipresent trees. In a situation

which cost him the 1955 Open, Ben Hogan needed three swats with a wedge just to extricate his ball from the rough, and it is alleged that Arnold Palmer unintentionally forfeited the 1966 edition when he continually mishit mid- and long-irons out of the tall grass. These facts, combined with moisture-laden fairways which offer no roll and tiny greens, mean Lakeside plays much longer than the card would indicate for both amateurs and pros.

As related earlier, the 1955 and 1966 Opens were memorable events. In 1955, Hogan looked to be well on his way to claiming yet another

OLYMPIC COUNTRY CLUB
SAN FRANCISCO, CALIFORNIA

HOLE	YARDAGE	PAR			
1	533	5	10	422	4
2	394	4	11	430	4
3	223	3	12	396	4
4	438	4	13	186	3
5	457	4	14	417	4
6	437	4	15	157	3
7	288	4	16	609	5
8	137	3	17	522	5
9	433	4	18	347	4
OUT	3,340	35	IN	3,486	36
			TOTAL	6,826	71

TEES	LENGTH	PAR	RATING
CHAMPIONSHIP	6,826	71	74.0
MIDDLE	6,496	71	72.1
FORWARD	6,157	76	76.2

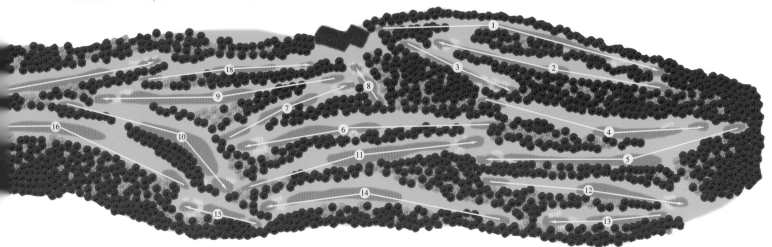

At less than 400 yards, the second hole depends on unusual fairway slopes and a well-protected green to defend itself.

The tee shot on the par-3 third hole must find the small, well-bunkered green 223 yards away.

Open trophy — it would have been his fifth. But Jack Fleck, otherwise destined to be a minor footnote in pro golf history, miraculously birdied the short but tough 18th hole to force a playoff. In the 18-hole battle the following day, Hogan again appeared headed for victory — until that horrible episode in Lakeside's rough. In 1966, Palmer, another golfing icon, was seven shots up on the field, led by Billy Casper, heading into the final nine holes of the championship. That bulge had diminished to five after 14 holes. On the par-3 15th, Casper made a 2 while Palmer bogeyed — the lead was now three. On the long par-5 16th, the swashbuckling Palmer went for broke, eventually carding another bogey to Casper's birdie. Another errant Palmer drive and corresponding Casper accuracy left the two tied after 72 holes. Even though Casper trailed Palmer by two shots at the turn during the subsequent playoff, he charged back to claim the title by four shots over a devastated Palmer.

Anyone who plays the Lakeside course can sympathize with the plight of Hogan, Palmer, and the innumerable others throughout the years who have been tempted to try to overpower this layout. Instead, a good score will result from intelligent course management: wise selection of club, line, ball flight, and so on.

That lesson is evident as early as the second hole, a mid-length par 4 that appears to drift to the left. Defying logic, however, the ideal shot pattern is a fade. On the fourth, you get a rude introduction to the "tunnel" effect of Lakeside's encroaching tree branches, which demands nothing less than a laserlike tee shot. Water hazards are nonexistent at Lakeside, and the fifth hole features the course's only fairway bunker. Branches again threaten wayward tee shots on the seventh, a short par 4, and the eighth, an otherwise straightforward par 3.

The closing holes at Lakeside begin with the par-5 16th. At more than 600 yards, only the legendary Bobby Jones is said to have ever reached it in two shots. The 17th, which the members play as a par 5, is shortened to a 440-yard par 4 for championship play. Heading into the prevailing wind, most players elect to hit their second shot just short of the green and hope for an accurate chip close to the hole, resulting in a tap-in par. The 18th, an unusually short par 4, presents all kinds of driving problems and has torpedoed the hopes of many players.

The 18th At Olympic's Lakeside

The 18th hole at the Olympic Country Club's Lakeside course is unremarkable on the card but extremely impressive in person. At less than 350 yards, a big hitter may go for the gusto with disastrous results. Trouble appears to lurk on the left, but the fairway is tilted to the right. Overhanging boughs will deflect any shot to the green attempted from outside the confines of the fairway. This hole has witnessed some great moments in golf history: most memorably in the 1955 and 1966 U.S. Opens when Hogan and Palmer, respectively, were caught here by their pursuers during regulation play and then soundly defeated in the ensuing 18-hole playoffs.

The 18th at Pebble Beach is one of the most spectacular finishing holes in all of golf.

PEBBLE BEACH

Golf Links

Architect: Jack Neville
Opened for Play: 1919

Ask almost any golfer, professional or amateur, where they would most like to play, and the answer will almost invariably be: "Pebble Beach." Tom Kite, who won the 1992 U.S. Open here, said: "I can't imagine a better place unless it's up there," pointing heavenward.

In 1919, developer Samuel Morse approached real-estate salesman Jack Neville to design a course for him along the shore of Carmel Bay. Of course, Neville was more than a real-estate salesman; he was a five-time California Amateur champion as well. Taking his responsibility seriously, Neville walked the property for weeks, mulling over potential routings, rejecting them, and starting again. Finally, he saw it. As he said later, "The golf course was there all the time. All I did was find the holes." He asked his friend

Right from the first hole, Pebble Beach is a special experience.

Douglas Grant to do the bunkering, and the rest is golfing history. Almost until the time of his death in 1978 at the age of 83, any proposed changes to Pebble Beach had to be approved by Neville.

Neville, while an obviously talented designer, had sense enough not to mangle what is maybe the most spectacular setting for a golf course in the world. The Monterey Peninsula, as Kite inferred after his Open win, is as close to heaven on earth as one can imagine. The waters of Carmel Bay, the sprawling dunes, the rugged hillsides of Northern California all combine to provide an unsurpassed golfing experience. In the words of Robert Louis Stevenson, who reputedly walked the grounds where the course now stands while formulating his next book, this area represents "the most felicitous meeting of land and water in creation."

"It was all there in plain sight," Neville told

A Tough Decision

Picking the toughest hole at a course like Pebble Beach must have been difficult...the first among equals. It is the consensus of most that the 464-yard ninth hole is the most difficult, sandwiched as it is between cliffs on the right and bunkers and gnarly rough on the left. The ever-helpful course guide recommends you "aim at the center of the fairway and hit it long, beware of the bunker to the left. Sidehill lies are the norm for long-iron second shots, so beware of the ocean right. There is a deep bunkered gully left and short that will punish a timid approach."

golf writer Herbert Warren Wind years later. "Very little clearing was necessary. The first three holes moved inland and then back toward the water. The next seven, with the exception of the short fifth, marched along the cliffs. The 11th through 16th looped inland and then back to the water. Then the 17th and the long 18th, which is quite possibly the best finishing hole in golf, edged home along the water." Jack Nicklaus has called 17 and 18 "the two most treacherous finishing holes on the courses where we play the Open."

The green of the miniscule par-3 seventh hole is a golfer's heaven on earth.

"The key to success here is in knowing the secrets of the course," says the course guide. "First, the astute golfer must know when to attack. The best opportunities come early in the round, on the relatively short second, third, and fourth holes. On six, the links start their five-hole trek along the 'cliffs of doom' — a section of the course best played conservatively, especially in the face of strong winds which can vary from a gentle breeze to a menacing gale."

PEBBLE BEACH GOLF LINKS
PEBBLE BEACH, CALIFORNIA

HOLE	YARDAGE	PAR			
1	373	4	10	426	4
2	502	5	11	384	4
3	388	4	12	202	3
4	327	4	13	392	4
5	166	3	14	565	5
6	516	5	15	397	4
7	107	3	16	402	4
8	431	4	17	209	3
9	464	4	18	548	5
OUT	3,274	36	IN	3,525	36
			TOTAL	6,799	72

Standing on the first tee, visitors must be forgiven if they are less than impressed. It is indisputable that the first five holes at Pebble Beach lack the heart-pounding thrill of the closing 13. But take advantage of this soft start, because as Lee Trevino has said, "If you're five over when you get to the sixth, it's a good time to commit suicide." The first hole is a medium-length par-4 dogleg right; the second a short par 5; the third a drive-and-pitch par 4 if you power a draw around the corner; the fourth an even shorter par 4 (albeit with heavy bunkering and the ocean flanking the entire right side — an omen of things to come); and the fifth hole is a 166-yard par 3.

The Pacific Ocean, in one of its nasty moods, appears to have taken a huge bite out of the right-hand side of the par-5 sixth hole. Even a solid drive will result in a blind second shot up to an unseen plateau. The seventh is a delicate 107-yard par 3 on calm days, but when the winds blow, it can play

TEES	LENGTH	PAR	RATING
BACK	6,799	72	74.4
MIDDLE	6,357	72	72.1
FORWARD	5,197	72	71.9

several clubs longer. The view from the tee is breathtaking as surf pounds against the boulders surrounding the green.

Holes eight through 10 are murder. On the 431-yard eighth, aim at the chimney in the distance and hope you can hit it 240 down the middle. Then you are faced with a mid- or long-iron shot across a chasm that devours most of the fairway and undoubtedly thousands of balls. It probably doesn't help to know that Nicklaus calls this the most challenging second shot in golf. Number nine is a brawny 464-yarder sandwiched between cliffs and rough and bunkers that is without a doubt the toughest hole on a very tough course. The back nine kicks off with a 426-yard bully with the beach delineating its right boundary and bunkers its left. The 384-yard 11th, the 202-yard 12th, and the 392-yard 13th provide some breathing space before you hit the par-5 14th, the No. 1 handicap stroke hole at Pebble Beach. Once through it, enjoy 15 and 16 before the knee-trembling finishing holes.

Pebble Beach welcomed Bing Crosby's famous "Clambake" Pro-Am back in 1947 and remains one of the three sites for the event, now called the AT&T Pebble Beach National Pro-Am. In addition, Pebble Beach has been the site of many championships: the U.S. Amateurs in 1929, 1947, and 1961; the PGA Championship in 1977; the Nabisco Championship in 1988; and the U.S. Opens in 1972, 1982, and 1992. The course is also scheduled to have the Open in the year 2000, the 100th playing of the championship.

The approach shot on the par-4 eighth hole is a golfer's gut check. You must cut off as much of the ocean as you dare!

———— Pinehurst, North Carolina ————

PINEHURST NO. 2

Architect: Donald Ross
Opened for Play: 1907

The year: 1900. It was a pivotal time in golf. James Walker Tufts, a soda fountain magnate, had heard about Donald Ross — a talented young golf professional up in Boston — who, it seemed, had a certain ability in course architecture. Tufts, who had purchased about 5,500 acres of North Carolinian timberland five years previously to establish a resort, was in need of such a talent. Ross, he figured, could preside over the existing nine-hole layout while designing a few more holes on which the tourists could while away the hours.

So Tufts invited Ross, who had studied golf at St. Andrews with Old Tom Morris, to come down during the winters. (Ross continued to work at Oakley Country Club, later the Essex, in Boston for several more summers.) Thank all the golfing gods that he accepted the invitation! It was at Pinehurst that the man many consider the greatest golf course architect of all time created what he himself considered his masterpiece: No. 2.

Ross, originally from Dornoch in Scotland, stayed at Pinehurst as the professional and later as the golf manager until his death in 1948. Along the way, he found time to design more than 400 courses in North America; it has been reported that by 1925, three thousand men were employed annually in the construction of his courses. He also maintained his status as a fine player during this time, winning three North and South titles (coincidentally held at No. 2) and claiming two Massachusetts Opens, four top 10 U.S. Open finishes, and an eighth-place finish at the 1910 British Open.

So Ross redesigned Tufts' rudimentary nine holes and added nine more: This was Pinehurst No. 1. Then he began what would become his life's work: No. 2. Although this course opened for play in 1907 at about 5,800 yards, Ross continued to fine-tune it almost daily until his death. Now recognized as one of the true works of genius in course architecture, No. 2 (what an unfortunate moniker!) plays to more than 7,000 yards. Its distinctive features included small, sloping greens, deep bunkers, loose sandy soil, and rough accents of wiry, native grass. In 1935, the sand greens were replaced with greens

At 184 yards, the ninth hole is the shortest par 3 at Pinehurst No. 2, Donald Ross's masterpiece.

PINEHURST NO. 2
PINEHURST, NORTH CAROLINA

HOLE	YARDAGE	PAR			
1	398	4	10	582	5
2	444	4	11	439	4
3	337	4	12	416	4
4	547	5	13	383	4
5	458	4	14	432	4
6	210	3	15	203	3
7	402	4	16	509	5
8	486	5	17	187	3
9	184	3	18	437	4
OUT	3,466	36	IN	3,587	36
			TOTAL	7,053	72

TEES	LENGTH	PAR	RATING
BLUE	7,053	72	74.1
WHITE	6,354	72	71.4
RED	5,863	74	74.2

composed of grass, which had become increasingly popular across North America.

In *The Golf Course,* the excellent reference book by Geoffrey Cornish and Ron Whitten, No. 2 is described as "a brilliantly deceptive form of strategic design. The course appeared to be straightforward. Its fairways were not particularly wide, but there was little rough. The greens were small and undulating, but very few of them were protected by more than a single bunker. But the illusion soon vanished once a round at Pinehurst No. 2 was begun. A ball off the fairway was either in the pines on a mat of pine needles or on the soft sandy soil cluttered with clumps of wiry 'love' grass. An errant driver at Pinehurst seldom found a good lie. And the greens required a great deal of concentration. Some bunkers were well forward of the green, and the careless player could find his approach land over the bunker but short of the putting surface. Many holes had only one bunker at the corner or side of the green. Yet to follow one's natural inclination and play away from the bunker was often a mistake. Ross counterbalanced most bunkers with greenside mounds and hollows, most of which posed more difficult recovery problems than the sand."

Pinehurst No. 2 does not take one's breath away with spectacle such as Pebble Beach nor does it humble the player with tradition in the manner of St. Andrews. It is the very epitome of subtlety. Indeed, many players who encounter it for the first time are dismayed by its seemingly benign nature. No. 2 is not an ax murderer; it is a pickpocket, a cat burglar which steals strokes from right under your nose.

The 16th is a short par 5, but the green is tucked behind the only water hazard on the course.

The Toughest Hole At Pinehurst No. 2

The No. 1 stroke hole at Pinehurst No. 2 is the 458-yard, par-4 fifth hole. "The hardest hole on the course, bar none," says the course guide. "It's long, the green is well bunkered, and there are few level lies from the fairway. The right side of the fairway makes for an easier approach, as you can run the ball up from that angle, but the hole also plays longer from that side."

Ross himself said his shifty greens and links-style mounding made "possible an infinite variety of nasty short shots that no other form of hazard can call for. Competitors whose second shots have wandered a bit will be disturbed by these innocent-appearing slopes and by the shots they will have to invent to recover." His greens are notable for sloping from front to back and side to side — to provide an actual target smaller than it appears and to reward the exact approach dictated by the hole. He called the course "the fairest test of championship golf I have ever designed."

The world's best players have challenged Pinehurst No. 2 and will continue to do so at the 1999 U.S. Open. The competitive opportunities predate World War I. Highlights include the 1936 PGA Championship, 1951 Ryder Cup Matches, 1962 U.S. Amateur, 1991 and 1992 Tour Championships, and the 1994 U.S. Senior Open. The North and South Amateur has been contested at Pinehurst without interruption since 1901, and No. 2 has hosted its share.

Ross would build two more courses at Pinehurst prior to his death. Since that time, four more have been added, all fine examples of architecture in their own right. But there will never be another No. 2.

The difficulty factor of the par-4 14th hole at Pinehurst No. 2 lies not only in its length of 432 yards, but also from the bunkering which appears to be tight to the green but in fact is some 20 yards short of the putting surface.

Pine Valley has been called "the hardest," "the toughest," but it is indisputably the best. Here is the par-4 12th hole.

——— *Clementon, New Jersey* ———

PINE VALLEY

Golf Club

Architects: George Crump, Harry Colt
Opened for Play: 1919

Golf Digest started ranking courses numerically in 1985. Guess who has been No. 1 ever since? Since you're reading this chapter, you only get one guess.

Pine Valley Golf Club rode its reputation for being the most difficult golf course into international legend for decades. But the focus on how tough it was deterred most golfers from examining the preeminence of its routing and design characteristics. Only since architectural experts in golf magazines and elsewhere started emphasizing that the course in New Jersey's densely forested sand hills deserved just as much respect for the quality of its design have golf aficionados taken a closer look.

"Even before it formally opened as an 18-hole course in 1919, Pine Valley had earned a phenomenal reputation, not only among golfers,

He Knew When To Quit

Knowing your limitations is one sign of a good golfer. For years, the story has been circulating around the Pine Valley clubhouse that, several decades ago, a talented local amateur with a good knowledge of the course started off birdie-eagle-ace-birdie — six under par after only four holes! The daunting prospect of maintaining such a pace convinced him to retire to the clubhouse for a refreshment, or several, while he pondered his predicament. His strategizing lasted until darkness, and the accumulated effect of those "refreshments" made completing the round impossible. He had won a battle, but Pine Valley won the war.

but among golf architects," says the definitive book *The Golf Course,* by Geoffrey Cornish and Ron Whitten. "Travis, Tillinghast, and Flynn all visited the course and were enthusiastic about its possibilities. Donald Ross and Charles Blair Macdonald both pronounced it the greatest course in the country."

The authors of *The Golf Course* point out astutely that these pillars of golf course design realized immediately that George Crump, a millionaire Philadelphia hotelier, and English course architect Harry Colt had rewritten many principles of course design. The landing areas were artificial islands of closely mown grass adrift in a sea of forest, sandy wasteland, scrub brush, water, and other potential misfortunes. Woe to the ill-fated golfer who failed when called upon to carry these waste areas from the tee or on an approach. The introduction of Pine Valley "marked the zenith of the penal school of golf course architecture in America," say Cornish and Whitten. "No course quite like it has been built since, and no course has ever been as demanding of every stroke."

The herculean, 436-yard par-4 16th at Pine Valley, a course once called "George Crump's 184-acre bunker."

Crump so believed in the potential of Pine Valley that he sold his Colonnades Hotel in Philadelphia, some 20 miles distant, and literally moved onto the site. He started the routing and supervised the removal of tens of thousands of trees before inviting Colt to help him complete the project. Although Crump was likely unaware of the coincidence, his property presented an uncanny resemblance to Sunningdale, Colt's home course in England. Colt pitched in, but four holes still remained to be built in early 1918 when Crump died unexpectedly. Brothers Hugh and Alan Wilson came to the rescue, completing holes 12 through 15 in a manner totally consistent with the existing 14.

Crump would have been proud of the formidable integrity of his project: The par-70 barrier was not broken until 1920 and then not again for almost another 20 years. No major tournament has ever been held here. The reasons cited include lack of space for spectators and parking and, no doubt, the reluctance of the members to open the gates. Another unacknowledged reason may include deference to the egos which would most certainly be demolished should any group of world-class players compete over Pine Valley's 6,765 yards. Only two events of note, the Walker Cups of 1936 and 1985, have been contested here, and both were won by the U.S. While the scores are duly recorded, the psychological damage was no doubt incalculable.

It is easy, perhaps inevitable, to fall into the

The 17th hole illustrates a typical Pine Valley challenge: 344 yards uphill to a green almost totally encircled by sand.

trap of portraying Pine Valley as the monstrous child of some psycho amateur architect with more money than brains. But the course presents a challenge to golfers of most abilities (although high-handicappers should take up another sport immediately upon being invited to play here) and should be respected for that reason alone. The holes are architecturally and aesthetically wonderful. Perhaps the most recognizable hole is the seventh, one of two par 5s at Pine Valley. Once again, the unfortunate name of the major design characteristic here dampens your enthusiasm. "Hell's Half Acre" is a bunker which stretches about 150 yards along

the edge of this 585-yarder which, club legend has it, has never been reached in two shots.

Pine Valley's par 3s are exceptional. Once one overcomes the churning fear that missing the green is not necessarily fatal, one can admire the way the target is defined and the golfer's task is determined. The third is typical: At 185 yards, the teeing ground and the green are the only grassed areas in sight. The fifth stretches more than 225 yards from an elevated tee to a similarly elevated green. In between is the usual Pine Valley buffet of potential humiliation: a water-filled ravine edged with brush. And did we mention the green is all but surrounded by Crump's impression of the Sahara? The front bunker on the 145-yard 10th often forces players to hit out of it back toward the tee, and the 185-yard 14th features an island green. Why not think of them all as short, but challenging, par 4s?

Bernard Darwin, one of the greatest golf writers, once remarked that Pine Valley is "an examination in golf." For those few fortunate enough to play what many experts call the best course in the world, he might have added "and of human nature."

PINE VALLEY GOLF CLUB
CLEMENTON, NEW JERSEY

HOLE	YARDAGE	PAR			
1	427	4	10	145	3
2	367	4	11	399	4
3	185	3	12	382	4
4	461	4	13	446	4
5	226	3	14	185	3
6	391	4	15	603	5
7	585	5	16	436	4
8	327	4	17	344	4
9	432	4	18	424	4
OUT	3,401	35	IN	3,364	35
			TOTAL	6,765	70

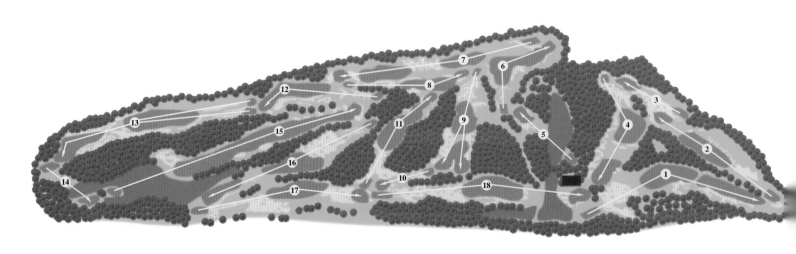

——— *Plainfield, New Jersey* ———

PLAINFIELD

Country Club

Architect: Donald Ross
Opened for Play: 1921

One thing that seems to separate Plainfield from many other courses that show up in the "best of" lists is the enduring commitment to being a family club. In fact, although Plainfield has been in *Golf Digest*'s Top 100 list since it was initiated in 1969, the president's comments in the club's centennial publication makes a point of emphasizing that Plainfield is "a family club kept alive and nurtured with the idea that parents, their youngsters, and their seniors can and should enjoy its facilities. All of us today enjoy a spirit instilled decades ago which celebrates our families and those of our fellow members. The foresight of those who have gone before us has left us a heritage of people and place."

Judging from the content of that publication, there is no doubt that Plainfield owes much to its founders, its staff, and the caliber of its

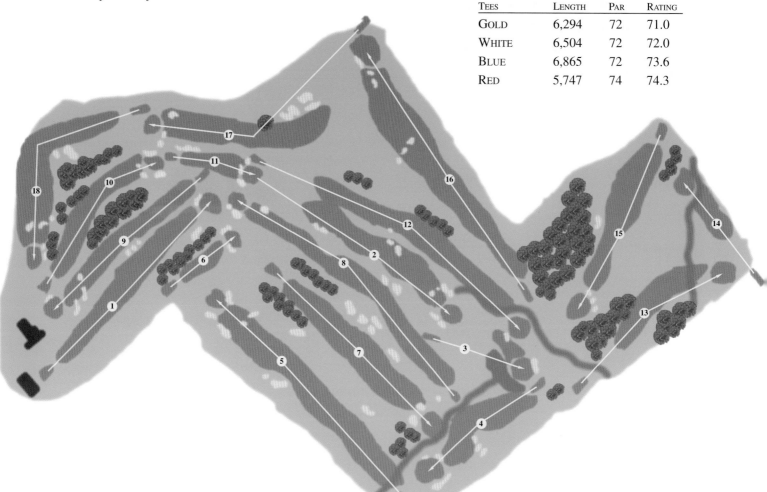

Tees	Length	Par	Rating
Gold	6,294	72	71.0
White	6,504	72	72.0
Blue	6,865	72	73.6
Red	5,747	74	74.3

PLAINFIELD COUNTRY CLUB
PLAINFIELD, NEW JERSEY

HOLE	YARDAGE	PAR			
1	431	4	10	360	4
2	450	4	11	147	3
3	179	3	12	585	5
4	331	4	13	442	4
5	525	5	14	224	3
6	141	3	15	371	4
7	458	4	16	554	5
8	497	5	17	419	4
9	367	4	18	384	4
OUT	3,379	36	IN	3,486	36
			TOTAL	6,865	72

membership. A group of Wall Street brokers established what was known as the Hillside Tennis Club in 1890. Five years later, bowing to the raging popularity of golf, the club relocated a couple of miles down the road. Finally, in 1897, the club found its present location and hired Tom Bendelow to design an 18-hole course which opened in 1898.

Those early directors also had the sagacity in 1916 to hire Donald Ross to design a layout over the existing property and an additional parcel. Although construction began in 1917, World War I intervened and building did not resume until 1920. Now the members of Plainfield Country Club had 27 holes spread out over 187 acres. No less an authority than Walter Hagen called it "one of the greatest golf courses I ever played," despite the fact that it was less than 6,300 yards long.

The caliber of the volunteers with which Plainfield was blessed in those early days is typified by Leighton Calkins, president from

1908 until 1914. Calkins was a president of the state golf association, a member of the executive committees of both the Metropolitan Golf Association and the United States Golf Association, and the mayor of Plainfield. Of interest to modern-day golfers is the fact that the handicap system he devised formed the basis for the one used today, and he is credited in some circles with coining the term "par."

Architectural experts continually cite Plainfield as one of Ross's best works. Although some criticize the ill-advised addition of ponds around the property, they agree that the overall design and especially the bunker complexes are close to perfect. "But most memorable are the greens, seven of which are perched atop knolls, often demanding an approach to a semi-blind pin placement," says a club publication. "Many are dramatically contoured, featuring severe slopes, swales, terraces, and crowns. The term 'strongly fortified' has been used to describe them — and that may be an understatement!"

Aside from the out-of-context ponds, the

Aficionados of traditional course architecture will be fascinated by Ross's greens and bunkering, such as on the par-5 12th hole.

The par-4 seventh hole at Plainfield is almost 460 yards from the blue tees.

The Worst 69

Johnny Kinder was the second golf professional at Plainfield Country Club. More than just the club pro, he was an outstanding player, winning the New Jersey State Open three times and the state PGA Championship four times. O. B. Keeler, a great golf writer, once wrote an article about Kinder called "The Worst 69 in the History of Golf." It was about how Kinder was on the verge of breaking the course record at Pinehurst No. 2 when he "blew up" on the last three holes to finish with a 69.

club contends that little has been done to detract from Ross's original inspiration. Even the renovation of three holes, now called the "Tunnel" (13, 14, 15), was overseen by Ross in 1927. Pushing back tees over the years now means that Plainfield can stretch to more than 7,000 yards, although that length has only been seen during major championships. It is during such events that Plainfield's nickname, the "Green Monster," truly applies.

In the 1978 U.S. Amateur, more than 200 of the country's finest amateurs arrived to try their hand at match play. Early favorite Jay Sigel bowed out quickly while teenage sensation Bobby Clampett, fresh from winning the Western Amateur and being low amateur in the U.S. Open, took Scott Hoch to 20 holes in a marvelous match. "The match was even going to the 18th hole, when Hoch hooked his drive into the woods but recovered with a soaring 8-iron to the green to force over-time," says the club's history. "On the first extra hole, it was Clampett's turn for the miraculous. After pushing his first shot to the edge of the sixth green, and forced to take a stance well below the ball, Clampett hit a green he wasn't able to see with a wide hook that kept the gallery buzzing well after the match had ended." Unfortunately for Clampett, another errant drive led to Hoch closing him out on the following hole. The 36-hole final saw Cook, an Ohio State student, race to an 8-up lead over Hoch and then coast to a 5&4 victory.

Preparations for the national women's Open began years prior to 1987 when new tees were built on several holes. The nines were reversed to better accommodate spectators and television coverage. But all the preparation in the world could not have avoided the cruel jests of Mother Nature delivered that July: 98-degree temperatures, three inches of rain in 36 hours, and howling winds. The severe impact of the weather forced the extension of the event from four days to six. Damage caused by the weather and ruts carved out by carts on waterlogged fairways took almost two seasons to repair. Eventually, Laura Davies of England, Ayako Okamoto of Japan, and American JoAnne Carner met on the Tuesday in an 18-hole playoff. Davies' one-under-par 71 edged Okamoto by two shots and Carner by three to claim the championship.

The par-3 14th hole requires a mid- to long-iron approach over water.

——— *Hutchinson, Kansas* ———

PRAIRIE DUNES

Country Club

Architects: Perry Maxwell, Press Maxwell
Opened for Play: 1956

Prairie Dunes just doesn't belong here. Scotland, maybe. Ireland, perhaps. But certainly not Kansas, of all places. The lineage of this course owes much to the seaside links of Scotland and Ireland; little to anything remotely associated with Kansas, unless you take into account the vision and imagination of a handful of folks with surnames such as Carey and Maxwell. "Thank goodness for the foresighted founding fathers, the Careys and Perry Maxwell, who, after all, studied under Dr. Alister Mackenzie himself!" comments PGA Tour player Ben Crenshaw, a noted architect in his own right, in the club history.

Emerson Carey founded the Carey Salt Company based on a gigantic deposit of sodium chloride located under Hutchinson, Kansas. His four sons carried on the business and became dedicated golfers, so dedicated in fact that in the mid-1930s they commissioned Perry Maxwell

Cleverly designed and attractive bunkers, like these on the short third hole, add to the British feel of Prairie Dunes.

to design a course northeast of town. Maxwell, who had indeed worked under Mackenzie at Augusta National and designed Southern Hills in Oklahoma, immediately recognized a stunning property all but unique to North America.

"On his way into Hutchinson, he was very excited by the countryside," recalled his son, Press, who would build an additional nine holes at Prairie Dunes some 20 years later. "It seemed to him, as it did to many others, that this part of Kansas looked just like parts of Scotland. He thought that the area would be a wonderful site for a Scottish-type course in the valleys of the sandhills." Sure enough, some authorities have been quoted as saying that all Prairie Dunes needs is a firth to look just like a British Open venue. Visitors will have to visually substitute the seas of wheat for the Irish Sea; intractable yucca plant and plum thicket do an all-too-effective impression of gorse and heather.

If anything, Perry Maxwell was faced with an embarrassment of riches. "There are 118 golf holes here," he said surveying the rolling dunes.

TEES	LENGTH	PAR	RATING
BLUE	6,598	70/72	72.5
WHITE	6,153	70/72	71.2
RED	5,512	70/72	71.8
GOLD	5,035	70/72	69.0

PRAIRIE DUNES COUNTRY CLUB
HUTCHINSON, KANSAS

HOLE	YARDAGE	PAR			
1	432	4	10	185	3
2	161	3	11	452	4/5
3	355	4	12	390	4
4	168	3	13	395	4
5	438	4/5	14	370	4
6	387	4	15	200	3
7	512	5	16	415	4
8	430	4	17	500	5
9	426	4	18	382	4
OUT	3,309	35/36	IN	3,289	35/36
			TOTAL	6,598	70/72

A good drive can carry the dogleg on the short par-4 14th, providing a straightforward approach to another of Prairie Dunes' distinctive greens.

"All I have to do is eliminate 100." He hiked back and forth across the 480 acres the Careys had acquired for several weeks before routing what would eventually be an 18-hole course. Only nine holes would be built immediately, and that layout was widely known as the best nine-hole course in the country before Press Maxwell produced the additional nine in 1956.

Perry Maxwell's original nine survives largely intact today in the following holes: 1, 2, 6, 7, 8, 9, 10, 17, and 18. They and their nine younger brothers are characterized by what are called "Maxwell Rolls" — the severely undulating greens which were the

The Best Par 3?

The 10th hole is an exceptional par 3 with a punishing green surrounded by trouble: a brush-covered dune, a gaping bunker, steep drop-offs, and more bush. Members describe certain pin positions here as sadistic and advise that a bogey is nothing to be ashamed of. Perry Maxwell recognized that here was a jewel. "This is the most beautiful par 3 I have ever constructed," he said. "Cypress Point, St. Andrews, Pinehurst, and Augusta National have nothing to compare with it."

elder Maxwell's trademark. So recognized and respected was Perry Maxwell's mastery of greens-building that he was also called in to redo putting surfaces at Augusta National, Pine Valley, and The National Golf Links of America, among others. "The Pine Valley of the West," says Jack Nicklaus when speaking of Prairie Dunes because of its humiliating greens, its severe rough, its length, and those omnipresent intimidating dunes.

With all those weapons in its arsenal, Prairie Dunes does not need to rely on length to test players. The eighth hole has been singled out as one of the finest par 4s in the United States, yet it is only 430 yards long. Due to the impenetrable rough, little is gained by carrying the dogleg, and the aggressively contoured plateau green makes a two-putt anything but a certainty. Even the short par 4s are a study in architectural genius. Long drivers may be stymied by a variety of obstacles, such as huge cottonwood trees (No. 13), fairway bunkers hedged by yucca plants (No. 14), or plum bushes encroaching into the landing area (No. 18).

Joe Dey, at various times the head of the USGA and the PGA Tour, commented that Prairie Dunes constantly put him in mind of the great Scottish links. "The entire course is such an excellent example of the links concept," Dey said. "That is, that Prairie Dunes could be transported 'as is' from that beautiful prairie to the coasts of the Irish Sea or the North Sea, where the roots of the game will always be, and it would be right at home...a good logo to symbolize this course would be of a lone golfer standing deep in the rough looking for his ball."

The final word goes to the insightful Crenshaw, architect, golf historian, and player:

"Anybody who has ever visited Prairie Dunes will be treated to real golf; the kind that tests you in the most enjoyable manner, with your brains and your body. The holes tumble and toss and turn very quietly and naturally with the most properly placed bunkers telling you where and where not to go. Yes, this is golf of the first order."

The 390-yard 12th hole with its huge cottonwood tree encourages a lay-up off the tee.

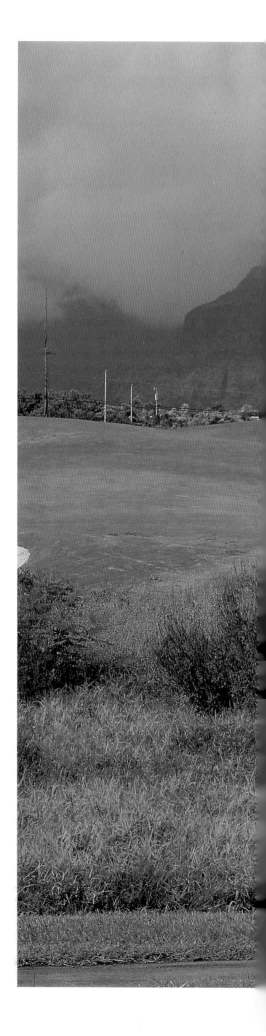

The Princeville Resort on the Hawaiian island of Kauai offers two great courses, each with its own personality. This is the par-4 fifth hole on the Prince course.

———— Kauai, Hawaii ————

PRINCEVILLE

Resort

Architect: Robert Trent Jones Jr.
Opened for Play: 1990

Where else in the world can a golfer find two of the world's best golf courses rolling through an ocean-bluff plateau with breathtaking mountain views? As a golf destination, few places can compare with Princeville Resort, named after a young 19th-century Hawaiian prince, Albert Edward Kauikeaouli Leiopapa A. Kamehameha. *Golf* magazine has honored the resort, proclaiming that the golf holes "aren't merely memorable — they're unforgettable."

Robert Trent Jones Jr., the designer of the 18-hole Prince course and the 27-hole Makai course, says that "in all the world, I never expect to find a more spectacularly beautiful place to build a golf course than Princeville." The man who designed more than 160 courses in 33 countries calls the Prince "one of the top five courses I've designed." In his book, *Golf by Design*, he notes: "Occasionally, an architect is fortunate to be presented

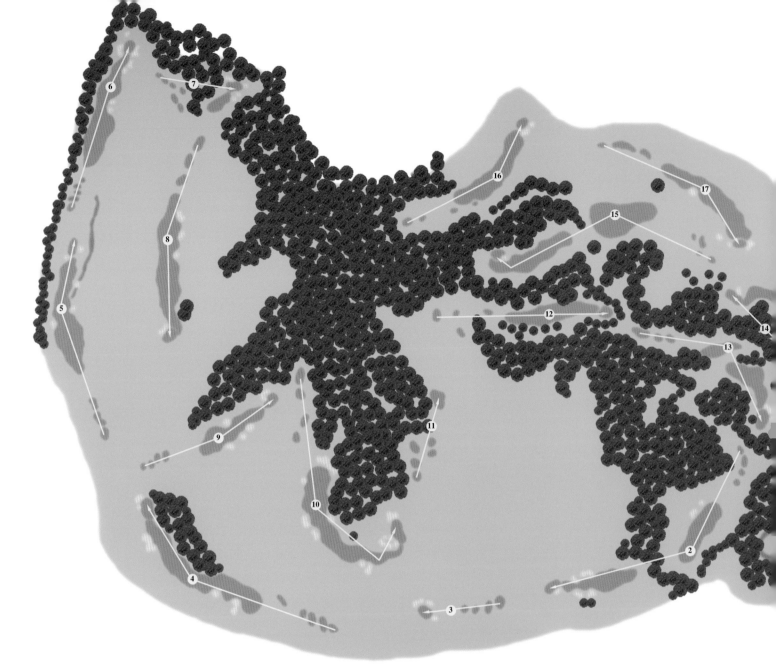

Princeville Resort
Kauai, Hawaii

HOLE	YARDAGE	PAR			
1	448	4	10	588	5
2	597	5	11	187	3
3	177	3	12	390	4
4	554	5	13	418	4
5	453	4	14	211	3
6	428	4	15	576	5
7	205	3	16	375	4
8	460	4	17	421	4
9	366	4	18	455	4
OUT	3,688	36	IN	3,621	36
			TOTAL	7,309	72

TEES	LENGTH	PAR	RATING
BLACK	7,309	72	75.3
BLUE	6,960	72	73.7
WHITE	6,521	72	71.7
GOLD	6,005	72	69.3
RED	5,338	72	72.0

with a magnificent site that presents tremendous opportunities. I have been blessed to work on several great pieces of dramatic property. Certainly, the bluffs overlooking the Pacific Ocean and the huge ravine, with waterfalls and streams amid the mature tropical vegetation, place the Prince course in that glorious assemblage."

While both layouts can stand on their own merits, it is the Prince's 18 holes that have impressed the golf cognoscenti around the globe. Since opening in 1990, this track has been consistently chosen among the top courses in the United States by *Golf Digest, Golf, Golfweek,* and *Western Links.* "The Pine Valley of Hawaii," gushed one golf writer. It spans 390 acres of rolling tableland bisected by tropical jungles, waterfalls, streams, and ravines. It has been called the most challenging course in the state, yet its multiple teeing areas should accommodate even the most casual golfers. A huge 13-acre practice facility includes a 1,200-square-foot putting green, a 1,200-square-foot

chipping green, and three different teeing locations which allow players to experience varying situations and wind conditions.

The signature holes at this bruising beast (a Slope rating of 145 and course rating of 75.3 from the "Black" tees, but you can't play from back there unless your handicap is five or less) are the seventh, 10th, 12th, and 13th. The par-3 seventh plays more than 200 yards from the tips and is reminiscent of the famous 16th at Cypress Point. The obvious difference is that the layout is reversed, with the lay-up area on the right side and the Pacific Ocean on the left. From the back tee, the ball must carry more than 200 yards into the teeth of the wind, although nine different tee decks gradually reduce that herculean effort down to a mere 98 yards from the forward tees.

The 588-yard, par-5 10th features a large ravine filled with tropical vegetation bordering the entire left side and fronting the

Like all Hawaiian courses, the Prince course is lush and beautifully conditioned, as typified by the opening hole.

More than 200 yards of jungle separates the tee and green of the Prince course's par-3 seventh hole.

green. Bunkers also line the entire right side of the hole with a huge cluster protecting the right side of the putting surface. While some pros might hope for a rare eagle by reaching the green in two shots, most players must realistically assess their chances and elect to go with a safe lay-up to the left or right of two large mango trees. The approach shot still must tackle a headwind while homing in on a wide but shallow green.

On the par-4 12th, the tee shot sails off a perch 100 feet above a slender fairway lined by dense jungle. If the player is lucky or precise enough to find the ribbonlike landing area, the Anini Stream comes into play on all sides of the green on the second shot. The green is surrounded by an amphitheater of ferns and other tropical foliage. The subsequent hole, a 418-yard par 4, is as difficult as it is beautiful. The target fairway is cut through tropical jungle to a landing area 200 yards away. A waterfall cascading behind the green fills Anini Stream, which meanders around the green and dissects the fairway just beyond the landing area; so beware.

No weak sister, the Makai course is comprised of three distinctive nine-hole layouts, each named for their distinctive characteristic: Ocean, Lakes, and Woods. Constructed in 1971, it was the first solo effort by Robert Trent Jones Jr. to be ranked in the top 100 courses in the U.S. Indeed, it continued to be ranked in that elite company for 16 straight years. For four years, it hosted the Women's Kemper Open, a prestigious LPGA event. In 1978, the World Cup was played here, and in 1990, the first Itoman LPGA World Match Play Championship was held at Makai.

Princeville Resort is recognized worldwide as one of the finest luxury destinations. In addition to its 45 holes of championship golf, the resort caters to every whim and desire. More than 20 tennis courts, including some that are lighted, provide the focus for the fully equipped tennis center. A full range of water sports is available, including kayaking, snorkeling, windsurfing, and scuba diving. Instruction is also available. Horseback rides amble across the spectacular Princeville Ranchland with dazzling views of ocean, waterfalls, mountains, and Hanalei Bay and Valley. The hotel itself boasts 252 guest rooms and suites, with a subtle Hawaiian influence. Exclusive shops, fine dining, and a complete health club and spa round out the Princeville Resort experience.

Each hole at the Princeville Resort is an aesthetic and golfing occasion. Pictured is the 428-yard sixth hole at the Prince course.

Sam Snead called the
shot on the par-5 openi
hole "one of the scari
drives at Rivier

—— *Los Angeles, California* ——

RIVIERA

Country Club

Architect: George C. Thomas, Jr.
Opened for Play: 1927

In the early 1920s, attests the official history of the Riviera Country Club, "the Los Angeles Athletic Club was without question the quintessential sports club in America. It housed the nation's most extensive facilities with a novel 12-story building...and the membership read like a Who's Who of American sports and business." But the closest this illustrious club could come to a golf course was the Sky-high Nine Hole Golf Course: an undulating putting green of billiard cloth over cunningly devised hillocks and hollows of modeling clay, flanked by nets for practicing full shots — on the roof of the Athletic Club!

As with many of the finest golf clubs over the years, one man and his vision brought Riviera Country Club to reality. Frank Garbutt was the vice president of the Los Angeles Athletic Club, and he would not rest until the club had a golf course that measured up to the rest of its facilities. In 1922, he found the perfect location in the Santa Monica Canyon near what is now Sunset Boulevard.

The par-3 fourth hole at Riviera is one of the best-known and most feared short holes in America. No less an authority than Ben Hogan once called this the greatest par 3 in the United States.

George C. Thomas Jr. was renowned as the finest amateur golf architect in America. When approached by Garbutt, Thomas had designed 25 courses and had not accepted a fee for any of them. But what the Los Angeles Athletic Club saved on Thomas's fee was more than compensated for by the cost of the course construction. The average cost to build a course in those days was about $70,000; Riviera cost more than three times that figure.

As opening day approached, Thomas was quoted as saying about his masterpiece: "It will be majestic, a thing of colossal beauty and still a golf course which will afford the maximum of pleasure to young and old, weak and strong. The dub player will have his chance to play his game just as much as the scratch player. There will be avenues of safety for the dub and carries of thrilling distances for the expert."

The clubhouse was equal in stature to the course over which it presided. Club historian Geoff Shackelford describes it as "a 46,000-square-foot masterpiece with the best imported Italian marble, beautifully hand-crafted furniture, and numerous comfortable lounge areas. The clubhouse also included 36 hotel rooms which were offered for temporary rental or, more commonly, as permanent apartments. Thus, the clubhouse was later named 'The Grand Hotel of Golf'" and remains one of the most recognizable structures in the game.

From its opening, Riviera was a favorite oasis for movie stars and other denizens of high society: Douglas Fairbanks and wife Mary Pickford, Harold Lloyd (who also had an Alister Mackenzie-designed nine-hole course in his backyard), W. C. Fields, Olivia DeHavilland, Clark Gable, Katharine Hepburn, Rita Hayworth...the list is exhaustive. Perhaps the most colorful story from the early era involves Howard Hughes, who apparently played all his golf at Riviera after being asked to leave nearby Bel-Air for landing a plane on the 14th fairway to join Katharine Hepburn for a golf game he was late for. Many more notables were competitors or spectators at the adjoining Riviera Polo Club and Equestrian Center. In later years, Riviera was the hangout for Jerry Lewis, Dean Martin (who said he played Riviera only on days ending with a "y"), Victor Mature, Gregory Peck, James Garner, Glen Campbell, Sammy Davis Jr., Peter Falk, and many others.

Despite devastating floods, storms, and earthquakes dating back to 1939, Riviera has persevered and now, after 70 years, maintains its place among the finest courses in the world. Since it played host to its first major tournament — the 1929 Los Angeles Open — Riviera has continued to delight and discompose the expert and the dub, just as George Thomas said it would.

In 1988, Riviera was purchased for $108 million by Marukin Shoji Company Limited of Japan. Norubu Watanabe, the president of Marukin who also oversees the operation of Riviera, made it clear to the members and

RIVIERA COUNTRY CLUB
LOS ANGELES, CALIFORNIA

HOLE	YARDAGE	PAR			
1	501	5	10	311	4
2	460	4	11	561	5
3	434	4	12	413	4
4	238	3	13	420	4
5	426	4	14	180	3
6	170	3	15	447	4
7	406	4	16	168	3
8	368	4	17	578	5
9	418	4	18	447	4
OUT	3,421	35	IN	3,525	36
			TOTAL	6,946	71

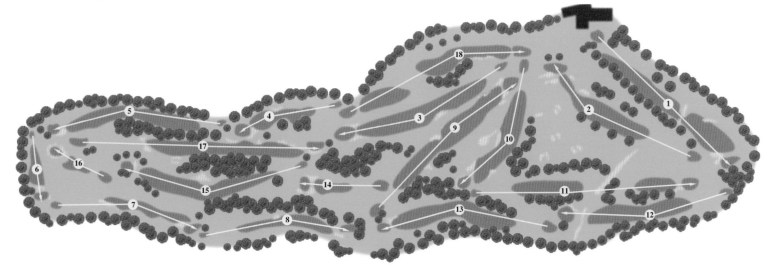

Par Is A Victory

Ranked perennially as one of the toughest holes on the PGA Tour, the second hole at Riviera was originally designed as a par 4 and plays as such during the Los Angeles Open. For the other 51 weeks of the year, it is played as a par 5 by members and their guests who are grateful they have been prescribed three shots, not two, to get to the green. They usually need all three — and frequently several more. Course architect George Thomas wrote of the second hole: "From the long or back tee, the wash which supplies the short driving carry is 125 yards away. The long hitter desiring a par by reaching the green on his second shot must place his shot accurately and make a still long pair of shots to avoid wing traps just short of the green. A second tee is provided for regular play which reduces the distance 30 yards. A fine long two-shotter from the back championship tee, this hole is a reasonable par from the regular tee."

the golfing world that the legacy of Frank Garbutt's vision was in good hands: "I want to honor the George Thomas design and do the same with the clubhouse — maintain the same classic, elegant design." Ironically, Watanabe came away from his first visit to Riviera — as a spectator at the L.A. Open — with but one wish: to play the course.

Riviera has played host to numerous prestigious championships, beginning with the 1929 L.A. Open. Through 1996, it had been the site of 35 Los Angeles Opens. In addition, Ben Hogan won the 1948 U.S. Open and Hal Sutton claimed the 1983 PGA Championship at Riviera. In 1998, Riviera will celebrate the 50th anniversary of Hogan's win by hosting the U.S. Senior Open.

One of the finest and most recognizable finishing holes in golf is the 447-yard 18th at Riviera.

If the character of a golf course is determined by the quality of its par 4s, then Riviera is elevated by its 431-yard 12th.

Designed by Donald Ross, Scioto Country Club in Ohio was made famous by Bobby Jones and Jack Nicklaus. Here is the par-3 17th.

———— *Columbus, Ohio* ————

SCIOTO

Country Club

Architect: Donald Ross
Opened for Play: 1916

James Hamill, Scioto's first president, was researching several courses prior to hiring an architect when, as he offhandedly remarked upon his return, "I stopped at Pinehurst to see Donald Ross." It was a fortuitous sidetrip. Ross, who is credited with over 400 designs and renovations, is widely recognized as the finest course architect of all time. His resume includes Pinehurst No. 2, Oak Hill, Oakland Hills, Seminole, and Interlachen.

Scioto took its place on the world's golfing stage through the heroic effort of Bobby Jones, who had the good grace and exceptional timing to squeak by Joe Turnesa by one shot to win the 1926 U.S. Open, the first major championship at the course. Jones, hailed at home and abroad as the finest golfer ever to swing a club, had arrived at Scioto directly from winning the British Open at Royal

The second hole, a mighty 438-yard par 4, has been called one of the best 18 holes in America.

The second hole, a mighty 438-yard par 4, has been called one of the best 18 holes in America.

Lytham and St. Anne's in England. Thus, by adding the U.S. title to his list, he identified Scioto as the venue where he had claimed an unprecedented "world championship" by winning both Open titles in the same year.

Ironically, Jones would indirectly have a hand in another major event hosted by Scioto: the Ryder Cup. It was immediately following the 1926 British Open that a dozen American players stayed on for an unofficial match against a similar number of Britons; the one thing they all had in common

was that they had lost to Jones. Sam Ryder, an English seed magnate, proposed sponsoring the match as an official event on an ongoing basis. Going into the 1931 edition, the Americans and the Brits had each won one match. Scioto was selected to play host to the rubber match which the home team won handily.

In addition, Scioto has played host to the 1950 PGA Championship (won by Chandler Harper) and the 1968 U.S. Amateur (won by Bruce Fleischer).

"He plays a game with which I am not familiar." Jones's famous words were spoken about the man who would use Scioto as a

SCIOTO COUNTRY CLUB
COLUMBUS, OHIO

TEES	LENGTH	PAR	RATING
BLUE	6,921	71	73.8
WHITE	6,398	71	71.5
GOLD	5,980	71	69.3

HOLE	YARDAGE	PAR			
1	410	4	10	424	4
2	438	4	11	365	4
3	377	4	12	545	5
4	188	3	13	435	4
5	438	4	14	238	3
6	527	5	15	428	4
7	380	4	16	425	4
8	505	5	17	191	3
9	162	3	18	445	4
OUT	3,425	36	IN	3,496	35
			TOTAL	6,921	71

The par-5 eighth at Scioto may not be long at 505 yards, but the prospect of going for the green in two can be daunting.

The Real Thing

The official history of Scioto, entertainingly written by sportswriter Paul Hornung, recounts a story wherein Gene Sarazen denies that the 220-yard 4-wood that resulted in a double-eagle on Augusta's par-5, 485-yard 15th hole in the 1935 Masters was the best shot he ever hit. In fact, Sarazen says, the best shot "was out of the Coke stand at Scioto." It happened during the 1931 Ryder Cup matches when Sarazen hit his tee shot on the fourth hole into a concession stand. "I saw an opening through the window," said Sarazen many years later. "The ball was resting on one of those grooves they have in concrete, and I knew the way it was resting that it would bounce up when I hit it. The ball went right through the window and onto the green about 10 feet from the cup, and I dropped the putt for a three."

springboard on his way to becoming an even bigger icon than Jones himself: Jack Nicklaus. Scioto's professional, Jack Grout, happened to mention to Nicklaus's pharmacist father in 1950 that he was starting a junior program. Mr. Nicklaus told Grout that he had a 10-year-old boy who wanted to learn golf. "The day we started," Grout said, "the first little boy on the tee was Jackie Nicklaus. He was just another little boy, no different from the other 30 or 40 little boys who showed up." That would soon change with Grout's tutelage, endless practice, and the opportunity to play Scioto's challenging layout.

"Scioto has always been a marvelous golf course," Nicklaus recollects. "It was a wonderful training ground for me. That's where my game was formulated, and I've played that way all my life. When you grew up on a Donald Ross golf course, you learned to play a variety of different kinds of shots. I learned to play left to right at Scioto. That's the way the golf course moves. Ross's greens were small greens, and you had to put a lot of elevation on your shots to hold those greens...Most of my ideas in how I play the game of golf, most of my ideas in golf course design came from this place."

Despite the wonderful Ross design, time and technology meant that Scioto was ready for a facelift in the early 1960s. Dick Wilson and Joe Lee were invited to update Ross's layout, a decision that was not taken lightly. Rather than bastardize the course, Wilson and Lee modernized the entire 18 holes, a revision that has remained true to Ross's legacy.

Take, for example, the second hole — the No. 1 stroke hole at Scioto is this 438-yard par 4. Wilson and Lee, the club's history

attests, "thought we should flatten the crowned fairway, but Ed Wilson (Golf Committee chairman) wouldn't hear of it. So it was left as before — obviously a wise choice since (it) was chosen by *Sports Illustrated* in 1966 as one of the 18 outstanding golf holes in America. Two traps were added to catch tee shots to the right, so they wouldn't go all the way down the hill. The former green was almost a square, with a ridge running through it. The new green is much more elevated, more severe as far as the breaks, and much larger."

The fifth hole is another 438-yard par 4, featuring a very narrow entrance to the green.

——— *North Palm Beach, Florida* ———

SEMINOLE

Golf Club

Architect: Donald Ross
Opened for Play: 1929

Think of Donald Ross. Think of the man's portfolio: Pinehurst No. 2, Oakland Hills, Plainfield, Oak Hill, Inverness, and literally hundreds more; called "the patron saint" of the American Society of Golf Course Architects; revered throughout the world of golf. Now think of how you would like the most knowledgeable experts in golf to refer to your course as "possibly Ross's finest creation."

Welcome to Seminole Golf Club. Oh, sorry, that "welcome" is just a figure of speech. While Seminole is indisputably a wonderful course, the club itself is just as indisputably ultraprivate, so your chances of experiencing Ross's masterpiece are extremely slim. Captains of industry mix with the crème de la crème of Palm Beach society both on the course and in the sprawling, Spanish-inspired clubhouse. If you don't fit in either of those categories, forget playing here.

Witnessing the outcome, it is perhaps not unusual that the Seminole project was one of the very few — some say the only — job that Ross campaigned for actively. In the late 1920s, he was becoming quite comfortable just waiting around his Pinehurst home for the steady stream of offers. But he was intrigued by the North Palm Beach property, the nature of which must have been undistinguished and puzzling to the layman. Two sandy ridges which traverse the site longitudinally were the only significant physical characteristics of the land when Ross surveyed it. Perhaps he sensed a challenge in finding the ultimate routing for 18 holes abutting Florida's Atlantic coastline. Whatever the reason, the result must have exceeded even his expectations.

"Appearances can be deceiving," wrote

SEMINOLE GOLF CLUB
NORTH PALM BEACH, FLORIDA

HOLE	YARDAGE	PAR			
1	370	4	10	382	4
2	387	4	11	403	4
3	501	5	12	367	4
4	450	4	13	168	3
5	195	3	14	499	5
6	383	4	15	495	5
7	432	4	16	399	4
8	235	3	17	175	3
9	494	5	18	417	4
OUT	3,447	36	IN	3,305	36
			TOTAL	6,752	72

TEES	LENGTH	PAR	RATING
GOLD	6,752	72	73.8
BLUE	6,480	72	72.0
WHITE	6,057	72	70.1
LADIES'	5,595	72	73.2

Herbert Warren Wind, the "patron saint" of golf writing. "Seminole, along with Pinehurst No. 2, is the quintessential Ross course. It may look mild and manageable — the fairways are wide, the rough is civilized, the undulations restrained, the greens large and candid — and because of its reasonable length from the standard tees the average player can sometimes salvage a par after a poorish drive. Nonetheless, after all is said and done, the course demands golf of the first order. Unless a player positions his tee shots carefully, he will not be able to regularly hit and hold the splendid variety of stiffly bunkered greens, and strokes will inevitably start to slip away fast."

The tee shot on the par-4 11th hole features a carry over water and a few of Seminole's 200 bunkers.

The 168-yard 13th at Seminole is a stunning, and tricky, par 3.

(It should be noted that a handful of top course architects murmur that the Seminole we know today is in fact the product of Dick Wilson, who allegedly was engaged to rework the layout after World War II.)

Whoever is responsible, the result is impeccable — and not just for the scratch player. Alternate tee positions lead to a variety of approaches to the greens, one hole even features two separate fairways, making the experience a great one for all handicap levels. This is a task not within the reach of many course designers, both today and historically.

That being said, should an invitation be made to play Seminole, defer the date until after you master bunker play. Originally boasting about 180 bunkers, the course now is inundated with more than 200 sand pits. Combine Ross's (Wilson's?) ingenious routing with 200 bunkers

and the coastal breezes and you are faced with a real challenge. Just ask Ben Hogan.

Hogan loved to practice at Seminole prior to competing at the Masters each April. "The wind is different here nearly every day, and that changes all the shots," Hogan once said. "I used to play Seminole for 30 straight days when I was preparing for the Masters, and I was just as eager to play it on the 30th morning as I was on the first. Seminole is a placement course. Most of the holes bend one way or the other slightly, and you must place your tee shot on the right side or left side of the fairway to have the best angle to the green on your approach shot. If I were a young man going on the pro tour, I would try to make arrangements to get on Seminole. If you can play Seminole, you can play any course in the world."

By Invitation Only

Seminole, this very posh, very exclusive venue, has never played host to a major event unless one counts the annual Pro-Am that was played there until 1960. The pot for the calcutta involved was rumored to reach into the hundreds of thousands of dollars every year. Every top player was invited; so many accepted that the PGA had to take exceptional steps with its schedule to avoid the competition. By all accounts, these fine players had to work hard to register a respectable score during these Pro-Ams. The course record, an unbelievable 60 in 1948, is held by Claude Harmon *(right)*, who was the club's head professional at the time.

The penultimate hole at Seminole is the 175-yard, par-3 17th.

———— Southampton, New York ————

SHINNECOCK HILLS

Golf Club

Architect: William Flynn
Opened for Play: 1931

Although the ultimate result is incomparable, Shinnecock Hills seems to have been the victim of some misconceptions from time to time. For example, it was thought for almost 60 years that Willie Dunn, a prevaricating Scot who served as the club's professional for many years, was the architect of the original 12-hole layout. Only in 1986 did a researcher uncover indisputable evidence that the designer was in fact Willie Davis, the head pro at Royal Montreal Golf Club in Canada. There also seems to be some confusion about whether Shinnecock or Chicago Golf Club can boast of having the first 18-hole layout in the country. And while several reputable authorities give credit for the modern layout to William Flynn, who also designed Merion Golf Club, other sources give the nod to Howard Toomey, Dick Wilson, or a mélange of the three.

Although it's not long at 408 yards, the par-4 15th features an intimidating tee shot and a tricky green protected by bunkers.

All this does little but serve as 19th-hole chatter after immersing oneself in a round at a golf course which has few rivals in this or any other country. In the final analysis, Shinnecock and, indeed, the game of golf itself as manifested in the United States validates the prescience of one of the club's founding members, William K. Vanderbilt. For it was he who, after witnessing a series of golf shots (ironically by the future Shinnecock professional Willie Dunn) in Europe in 1890, had opined to his cronies: "Gentlemen, this beats rifle shooting for distance and accuracy. It is a game I think would go in our country."

Serendipitously, those cronies were Edward Mead and Duncan Cryder. They lost no time in drumming up interest among a handful of fellow Southampton residents. One of those acquaintances, Samuel Parrish, negotiated the visit by Davis and, after one false start, found an expansive valley on the far end of Long Island for Davis to work his magic. The course was soon built using horse-drawn scrapers and the like, along with backbreaking labor by members of the nearby Shinnecock Indian reservation. The charming gabled clubhouse, which is still in use, was designed by Stanford White, who, among other achievements, drew the plans for Madison Square Garden and was shot dead by a chorus girl's jealous husband.

Some things — most significantly its justifiable fame as a golf course — about Shinnecock are not in dispute. While it was neck and neck with Chicago Golf as the first 18-hole course, it was definitely the first to incorporate, the first to have a clubhouse, and the first to have a waiting list for membership. Like Chicago Golf, it was one of the five founding members of the United States Golf Association.

What elevates Shinnecock above most of its peers is the inspired choice of location made more than 100 years ago. Although not on the ocean, this links-style layout exudes the atmosphere of a true links. More than two miles from the ocean itself, the Atlantic can be seen from points on the course, which is embraced

A Proud Beginning

Shinnecock did not wait long before casting its reputation before the world's best players. The 1896 U.S. Open and Amateur (the championships were held simultaneously in those days) traveled to Southampton with the result that James Foulis won the pro event and H. J. Whigham claimed the Amateur. That week can claim a proud notoriety for another reason: John Shippen, the son of an African-American father and a Shinnecock Indian mother, tied for fifth in the Open, an event in which he almost did not play. For prior to the first tee-off, some bigoted professionals confronted the president of the USGA and said they would not play if Shippen and Oscar Bunn, also a Shinnecock, entered the event. "Fine," was the USGA response. "Shippen and Bunn will play, even if no one else does."

The par-5 16th hole is called "Shinnecode" and encapsulates the course's splendid views and exemplary design.

Few courses offer as exhilarating an opening hole as this par 4 at Shinnecock Hills.

on the other side by Peconic Bay. Like those of its British forebears, Shinnecock roughs are fearsome and largely native to the area; the winds are fierce and unceasing. (Renowned architect Charles Blair Macdonald absorbed all these attributes when he designed Shinnecock's revered neighbor, the National Golf Links of America, in 1911.) "There is a sweep and a majesty to Shinnecock," says none other than Robert Trent Jones.

Although various amateur endeavors, such as the 1977 Walker Cup Matches, were invited to the links at Southampton, it was to be almost a century before the pros would again tread the fairways of Shinnecock. That 90-year hiatus was due to a combination of its reputation for ferocious difficulty, unpredictable weather, remote location, and the understandable reticence of the small and exclusive membership to open their club's doors to the hoi polloi. In the 1986 Open, only 17,000 spectators were allowed each day, about half the usual number.

A footbridge was constructed over the access highway to link the course with parking facilities, and a special train ran to Shinnecock from New York's Penn Station. The world's finest players sallied forth to do battle, knowing relatively little about their opponent. "Which holes played differently because of the wind?" a reporter asked Greg Norman. "One through 18," was his answer. In the end, 43-year-old Raymond Floyd had the low 72-hole score, but Shinnecock was the victor.

Thrilled by the experience, Shinnecock welcomed its next Open a mere nine years later to celebrate the USGA's Centennial.

TEES	LENGTH	PAR	RATING
RED	6,821	70	74.6
GREEN	6,248	70	72.1
WHITE	5,375	70	72.1

SHINNECOCK HILLS GOLF CLUB
SOUTHAMPTON, NEW YORK

HOLE	YARDAGE	PAR		HOLE	YARDAGE	PAR
1	391	4		10	412	4
2	221	3		11	158	3
3	456	4		12	469	4
4	409	4		13	372	4
5	529	5		14	447	4
6	456	4		15	408	4
7	184	3		16	542	5
8	361	4		17	169	3
9	411	4		18	426	4
OUT	3,418	35		IN	3,403	35
				TOTAL	6,821	70

———— *Tulsa, Oklahoma* ————

SOUTHERN HILLS

Country Club

*Architect: Perry Maxwell
Opened for Play: 1936*

Serendipity is defined as "an apparent aptitude for making fortunate discoveries accidentally." In that case, Southern Hills could
more aptly be named Serendipity Country Club.

What else would have possessed a couple of Tulsa businessmen
to approach Waite Phillips, millionaire founder of the Phillips
Petroleum Company, to finance a new country club on the outskirts
of town — in the midst of the Depression? Phillips, obviously a
sportsman with a whimsical streak, refused Bill Warren and Cecil
Canary the cash but turned the proposal back on them: If they
could locate 150 like-minded individuals who would kick in $1,000
each, Phillips would give them 360 acres! They did and he did.

Although Phillips termed the undertaking "ridiculous" and
seemed resigned to sitting back and watching it fall on its face, he

did intercede with the board when they were discussing potential course architects. (Serendipity was about to resurface.) It seemed he had become acquainted with a banker who dabbled in course design. As it turned out, his banker friend was no mere dilettante. Indeed, Perry Maxwell was perhaps the most prolific architect in the 1930s.

Maxwell was an associate of Alister Mackenzie and seldom strayed from America's heartland: Prairie Dunes in Kansas and Dornick Hills in Oklahoma top

his list of achievements. As impressive as his list of designs is the roster of courses which invited him to renovate holes or greens, including Augusta National, Pine Valley, The National Golf Links, Colonial, Crystal Downs, Merion, and Saucon Valley.

In true Maxwell style, Southern Hills does feature terrifyingly undulating greens in addition to its top-notch routing. "He didn't like to shape the land to fit his plan," his wife said. "The land should shape his plan." But those so-called Maxwell Rolls on the putting

The back nine at Southern Hills commences with a severe dogleg-right par 4, where an iron off the tee may be the wisest choice.

surfaces are just about the only hills here if you discount the elevation upon which the sprawling clubhouse reposes. Perhaps fittingly for the product of an architect who built most of his courses in the "Dust Bowl" states, the bunkers here are filled with fine, almost dustlike sand dredged from a local river which almost always guarantees a buried lie. Add the summer's oppressive heat and desiccating winds, and a bad day suddenly becomes reminiscent of the fall of Khartoum. In fact, the 1958 Open here was

nicknamed the "Blast Furnace Open," and no one smiled when they said that.

Just short of 7,000 yards for championship play, Southern Hills plays to a par of 70 when the top pros and amateurs come to visit and 71 for members. Maxwell's predilection for doglegs (six right and eight left), all of which are defined by mature trees these days, puts a tremendous emphasis on long, accurate driving. It has challenged the best players in the world, starting with the Women's U.S. Amateur in 1946. Ever since, Southern Hills has maintained a top-drawer reputation as a championship venue. It has played host to a dozen championships, including six majors. In addition to being the proposed site of the 2001 U.S. Open, this course has witnessed Opens in 1958, 1977, and 1996, and PGA Championships in 1970, 1982, and 1994. It also hosted the 1995 and 1996 Tour Championships.

In any discussion of Southern Hills, two holes are singled out for attention: the 12th and 18th. Ben Hogan and Arnold Palmer have called the 12th one of the great par 4s in the world. At 448 yards from the championship

The 405-yard third hole is a sharp dogleg left, requiring a tee shot to the right-center of the fairway.

Nine 3s In A Row!

In 1958, Tommy Bolt claimed the first U.S. Open played at Southern Hills with a one-under-par total, the same score Dave Stockton posted in winning the 1970 PGA Championship. Hubert Green managed to scratch out a two-under 278 in the 1977 Open. Members took fierce pride in how their course humbled the world's finest players — until Raymond Floyd *(right)* stepped to the tee in the first round of the 1982 PGA. Or rather until he stepped onto the sixth tee. Starting on that hole and continuing through the 14th, his scorecard read: 3, 3, 3, 3, 3, 3, 3, 3, 3 — nine 3s in a row on his way to an astounding 63!

Although Craig Stadler would doggedly pursue Floyd for the next three days, the eventual champion held on to register an eight-under-par 272 total, leaving his fellow competitors and Southern Hills members shaking their heads.

At 376 yards, the 10th hole is not long but requires an accurate drive and precise approach to one of the trickiest greens at Southern Hills.

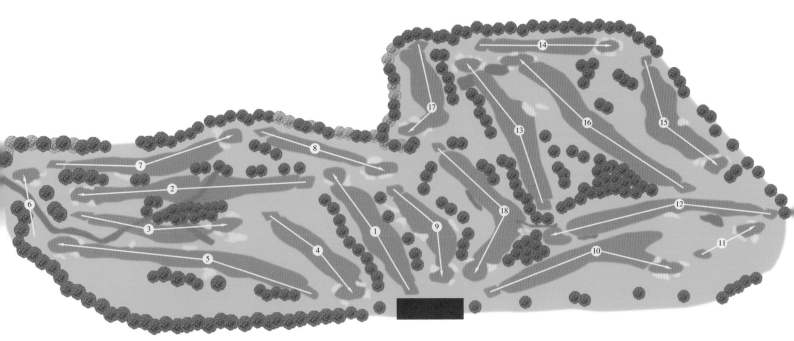

tee, this dogleg left rewards only a screaming blast off the tee. Although the dogleg crooks to the left, a slight fade will avoid the strategically placed bunker and thick trees which discourage anyone pondering a shortcut.

A water hazard, unseen from the fairway, cuts across the hole in front of a devilishly undulating green protected by more trees and bunkers. It was on 12 that Palmer had a chance to tie for the lead in the 1970 PGA. He hooked his ball into the water, took off his shoes, and splashed the semisubmerged ball into a bunker, making double-bogey. Palmer would never win a PGA Championship.

The closing hole produces raves: either pro or con. The 430-yard par 4 boasts a sinister smorgasbord of terror: a pond, bunkers, trees, heavy Bermuda rough...and that's just on the tee shot. After a perfect drive, you still face a long approach off a downhill lie to a huge, elevated, multileveled green with a terminal case of Maxwell Rolls.

Nine more holes have been added to Southern Hills, and they are, by all accounts,

SOUTHERN HILLS COUNTRY CLUB
TULSA, OKLAHOMA

HOLE	YARDAGE	PAR			
1	456	4	10	376	4
2	458	4	11	164	3
3	405	4	12	448	4
4	368	4	13	537	5
5	614	5	14	207	3
6	175	3	15	405	4
7	382	4	16	468	4
8	215	3	17	352	4
9	374	4	18	430	4
OUT	3,447	35	IN	3,387	35
			TOTAL	6,834	70

worthy additions. Although the expansion had been talked about since 1961, it took 30 years for the club to decide to proceed. Ben Crenshaw and Bill Coore were commissioned to do the project which, in a situation harking back to Southern Hill's origins, was approved in the midst of one of the worst economic downswings since the Great Depression. Serendipitously, both architects had grown up on courses designed by, who else, Perry Maxwell.

*Designer Robert Trent Jones
called upon New Jersey's Pine
Valley when creating the first
five holes at Spyglass Hill.
Here is the par-3 third hole.*

——— *Pebble Beach, California* ———

SPYGLASS HILL

Golf Course

*Architect: Robert Trent Jones
Opened for Play: 1966*

"If it were human, Spyglass would have a knife in its teeth, a patch on its eye, a ring in its ear, tobacco in its beard, and a blunderbuss in its hands. It's a privateer plundering the golfing main, an amphibious creature, half ocean, half forest. You play through seals to squirrels, sand dunes to pine cones, pounding surf to mast-high firs. It's a 300-acre unplayable lie," wrote Jim Murray, renowned sports columnist for the *Los Angeles Times.*

Appropriate comments for a course which took its name from Robert Louis Stevenson's *Treasure Island.* The holes themselves take their names from that famous book: Treasure Island, Billy Bones, The Black Spot, Blind Pew, Bird Rock, Israel Hands, Indian Village, Signal Hill, Captain Smollett, Captain Flint, Admiral Benbow, Skeleton Island, Tom Morgan, Long John Silver, Jim Hawkins, Black Dog, Ben Gunn, and Spyglass.

Murray's quote, which dates back to 1967, also provides a broad hint about the physical character of Spyglass Hill, which

SPYGLASS HILL GOLF COURSE
PEBBLE BEACH, CALIFORNIA

HOLE	YARDAGE	PAR
1	600	5
2	351	4
3	152	3
4	370	4
5	186	3
6	412	4
7	529	5
8	396	4
9	430	4
OUT	3,426	36
10	408	4
11	528	5
12	178	3
13	441	4
14	560	5
15	121	3
16	468	4
17	322	4
18	407	4
IN	3,433	36
TOTAL	6,859	72

TEES	LENGTH	PAR	RATING
BACK	6,859	72	75.9
MIDDLE	6,346	72	73.0
FORWARD	5,642	74	73.7

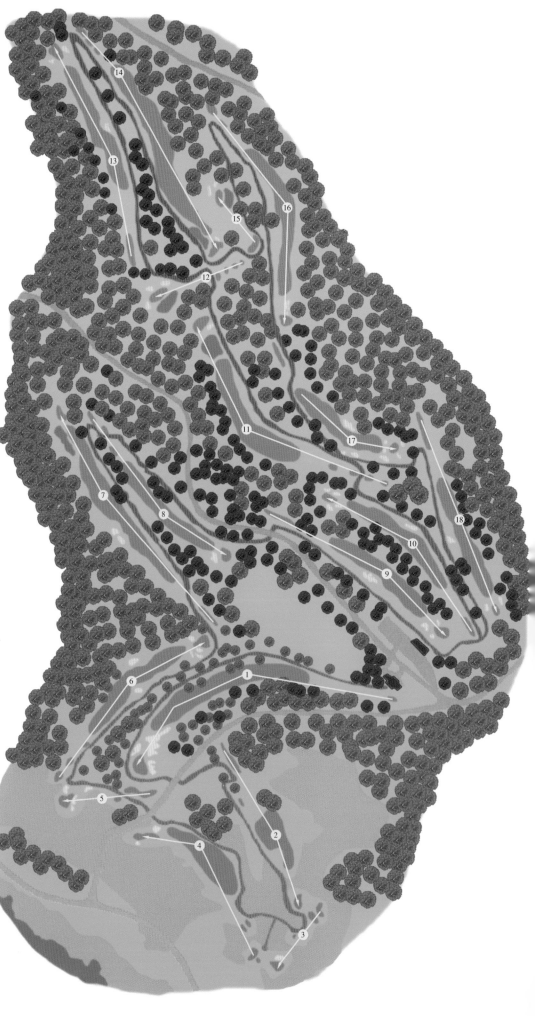

features five opening holes in spectacular links style and the remaining 13 in parkland. Robert Trent Jones, who designed Spyglass Hill in 1966 at the peak of his powers, said: "The first five holes were designed with Pine Valley in mind, and the remainder are designed like Augusta National with its majestic pines, lofty ocean views, elevated green, challenging bunkers in the landing areas, lakes to grab the errant shot, well-bunkered greens, and a challenging putting surface."

You don't have to wait long to experience the punitive power of Spyglass Hill. Off the first tee, a brutal treelined 600-yard par 5 swings from left to right, heading for the sea. The ideal tee shot will stay in the right-center of the fairway, setting up a mid- to long-iron shot to the bottom of the hill. A precise short-iron will stick on the well-bunkered green which slopes front to back.

The other four links holes continue to wend a path through the dunes, providing, on the shores of the Pacific, an experience as close to Scotland or Ireland as is possible on this side of the Atlantic. Number 2 is a medium-length par 4 which, at 351 yards, demands a long-iron struck to the left-center of the fairway, leaving a short approach to a narrow, sloping green. If the wind is up, the par-3 third hole requires careful club selection. The fourth, another sub-400 par 4, punishes anything less than two accurate shots. A 230-yard drive sets up a short-iron approach to a two-tiered green which slopes severely from front to back. "If you hit in the ice plant, the best bet is to take the shortest route out," says the course guide. Good advice, since this West Coast phenomenon combines the worst attributes of steel wool, rubber tubing, and barbed wire. Grab a sand

Uphill into the wind over the ice plant and bunkers, the par-3 fifth hole is no pushover.

A Great Pedigree

After Spyglass Hill opened, architect Robert Trent Jones said: "The first five holes were designed with Pine Valley in mind, and the remainder are designed like Augusta National with its majestic pines, lofty ocean views, elevated green, challenging bunkers in the landing areas, lakes to grab the errant shot, well-bunkered greens, and a challenging putting surface." Other than those few obstacles, this course is a breeze!

A unique feature of the par-3 12th is that the deeper the pin is on the green, the more water you must carry.

wedge, aim sideways, hope for the best, and cut your losses. The insidious ice plant is prominent on the par-3 fifth where club selection ensures there are as many 5s as 3s.

Now the routing takes you back into the Northern Californian forest, to holes which may not be as visually unique but which are no less difficult. From the sixth hole on, the course winds through the Del Monte Forest, and it seems that every hole plays uphill. This makes the 412-yard sixth play more like 440, and the blind second shot must be kept below the hole to ensure a reasonable chance at birdie. Par is a very reasonable score on this underrated hole. The eighth and ninth holes are monster par 4s, and any player who survives them in even par will breathe a huge sigh of relief.

The back nine meanders through woods and is interspersed with water hazards on the 12th, 14th, and 15th holes. The 178-yard 12th imitates the original and often-duplicated Redan, the 15th hole at North Berwick West Links in Scotland (the original 190-yard Redan has a ferociously angled green, hidden from the tee, which runs away from the shot;

instead of bunkers, the 12th at Spyglass Hill substitutes water). The 441-yard, par-4 13th is another sleeper. While the yardage gets your attention, the slightly uphill second shot always plays longer than it looks. The expansive green again slopes from front to back, and three putts from above the hole are common.

The 16th, the "Black Dog," is a treelined 468-yard par 4 which consistently rates as one of the toughest holes on the PGA Tour. The more cautious player will love a tee shot which lands in the left-center of the fairway. The more adventurous (foolhardy?) will gamble; the closer to the right, the higher the risk and resulting reward. From the tree in the middle of the fairway, it is a 225-yard carry to a small green. A missed second shot to either side will likely find a hazard.

Spyglass Hill is one of the three courses which plays host every winter to the AT&T Pebble Beach National Pro-Am, along with Pebble Beach Golf Links and Poppy Hills Golf Club. The tournament was originated by Bing Crosby, who was impressed with the difficulty of Spyglass Hill. So impressed, in fact, that he bet Jack Nicklaus he could not break par the first time he played it during a practice round for the 1967 event. Nicklaus, being Nicklaus after all, fired a two-under 70. Spyglass got its revenge during the first round of the tournament itself, when Nicklaus carded an indifferent 74. (He eventually won the event by five shots.)

Nicklaus remained on anything but friendly terms with Spyglass after that initial encounter, despite the fact he has won the event three times. "Pebble and Cypress [which was formerly in the rotation prior to Poppy Hills' addition] make you want to play golf," said Jack. "Spyglass Hill makes you want to go fishing."

The back nine at Spyglass Hill kicks off with "Captain Flint," a 408-yard par 4.

The par-4 14th hole at Troon
Golf and Country Club exhibits
all the attributes of desert golf
and outstanding design.

Scottsdale, Arizona

TROON

Golf and Country Club

Architects: Jay Morrish, Tom Weiskopf
Opened for Play: 1986

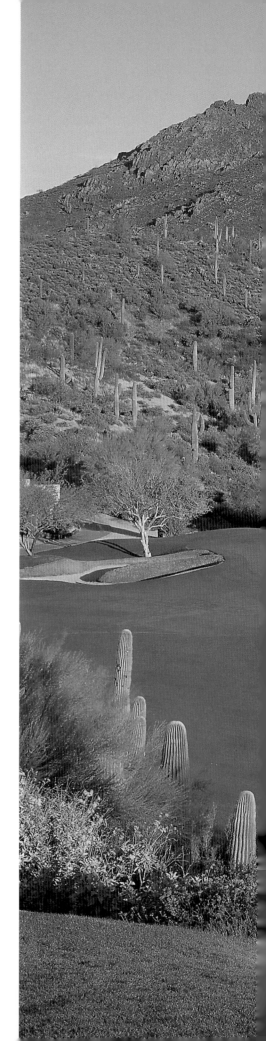

Troon Golf and Country Club is an 18-hole desert terrain course designed by Tom Weiskopf and Jay Morrish. While the name is less than innovative (it derives its moniker from Weiskopf's 1973 British Open win at Scotland's Royal Troon) and often leads to confusion with Troon North, another Weiskopf-Morrish layout in Scottsdale, the course itself has impressed since the day it opened. Only nine months after the first tee shot was struck, its par-3 15th hole was included in *Golf* magazine's "100 Greatest Holes in America." A year later, the same publication included Troon in its list of the 100 greatest courses in the world, an honor that continues to the present. *Golf Digest* selected it as the best new course of the year, and Troon then found a perennial spot on its "100 Greatest" roster.

The developer, Jerry Nelson, is as rare a bird to golf course development as a penguin is to Arizona. In an interview with *The Golf Club*, Weiskopf remarked that "a lot of clients want to get involved in the course they've hired you to design. Not Jerry Nelson. He just told us to do what we wanted out there. We never saw him after that until the course was finished." Even then, Nelson didn't really have a clue about what he had caused to be created. After Troon's name appeared on the "best of" lists, Nelson started getting congratulatory calls from friends. "I tried to be intellectual and detached about the whole thing, saying 'Oh yes, it's a very fine thing that has happened to us, I'm sure.' But the real importance didn't sink in for weeks."

Ranging from 5,167 yards from the forward tees to 7,041 from the tournament blocks, the available tees provide each level of player with unique challenges and varying degrees of difficulty. Nestled in the high Sonoran Desert at the base of the McDowell Mountains, the 2,400-foot elevation offers crisp, clean air and spectacular vistas. While the desert terrain may remind the first-timer of a moonscape, the target-golf concept of turf tees, landing areas, and greens interspersed with transitional areas on their way to real desert soon becomes as familiar as a conventional course. The layout was meticulously planned to harmonize with the fragile desert environment and to preserve natural resources. Visitors are reminded that the course is irrigated with reclaimed waste water and the ecosystem has been disturbed as little as possible.

The 15th (called Troon Mountain) is no doubt the best known of Troon's 18 holes, but many players recommend the 14th, a tremendous par 4 stretching 440 yards from the back tees. Wending its way through giant Saguaro cacti, "The Cliff" presents every one of Troon's challenges on one hole: elevation changes, jumbled castles of boulders, scrub, and sand. All this under the watchful eyes of the McDowell Mountains.

Befitting the Copper State, the focal point of Troon is the dramatic 48,000-square-foot copper-topped clubhouse, a contemporary structure of Southwestern

TROON GOLF AND COUNTRY CLUB
SCOTTSDALE, ARIZONA

HOLE	YARDAGE	PAR
1	430	4
2	460	4
3	541	5
4	296	4
5	215	3
6	463	4
7	207	3
8	507	5
9	411	4
OUT	3,530	36
10	395	4
11	532	5
12	400	4
13	189	3
14	440	4
15	139	3
16	347	4
17	629	5
18	440	4
IN	3,511	36
TOTAL	7,041	72

TEES	LENGTH	PAR	RATING
BLACK	7,041	72	74.8
BLUE	6,542	72	71.8
WHITE	5,929	72	69.1
RED	5,167	72	69.6

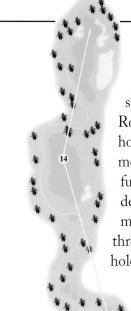

A Tough Decision

"There are no weak holes here, so it's a very tough decision," responded Troon head professional Roger Rockefeller when asked to identify the most challenging hole. When pressed, he picked the 14th as not only the most challenging but "one of the most aesthetically beautiful holes I've seen. From the tee, you have to carry some desert, a ravine, and boulders to get to the fairway. A driver might not be the club because you could hit your ball through the fairway, and then you would discover why this hole is called 'The Cliff.' It's at that point that the fairway drops 60, 70, 80 feet to another level. From the tees, it's a 2-iron or 4- or 5-wood off the tee, leaving about 165 to 180 yards into the green."

Don't be fooled by the scorecard on No. 10 — a host of disastrous opportunities lurks on this short par 4.

high-tech design which blends harmoniously with surrounding desert rock formation and provides members and their guests with stunning panoramic views. Housing a range of dining facilities from casual to elegant, men's and women's locker areas, lounges, libraries, a coed fitness center and pro shop, the clubhouse caters to the members' every need. A lagoon pool, adjacent barbecue, and lighted tennis courts complete the amenities.

Troon is a private, member-owned equity club offering world-class golfing and club facilities to a limited number of golfing and social members. Membership in this club is limited to property owners in the Troon community. No riffraff here. Applications for membership undergo a comprehensive review process by the membership committee, including background and credit checks, before submittal to the board for approval. A 10 per cent down payment of the current $80,000 initiation fee must accompany each application. For those who want to play at the invitation of a member, remember that "guest fees reflect the world-class status of the club," says a spokesman. World-class guest fees...what next?

Like its namesake at Scotland's Royal Troon, the par-3 13th "Postage Stamp" requires an accurate and decisive tee shot.

Although the Mountain course is better known, the Canyon course at Ventana Canyon presents its own unique challenges. Here is the par-5 18th.

—— *Tucson, Arizona* ——

VENTANA CANYON

Golf and Racquet Club

Architect: Tom Fazio
Opened for Play: 1985 (Mountain Course); 1987 (Canyon Course)

Designed by Tom Fazio, both the Mountain and Canyon courses have won numerous awards. A two-time *Golf* magazine Silver Medalist, the resort has also been honored by *Golf Digest,* as the best resort course in Arizona, and by *Golfweek,* as one of the best courses in the country.

A single round of golf explains the popularity of these courses. Perhaps the most photographed golf hole west of the Mississippi, the celebrated Mountain No. 3 plays across 107 yards of cactus and canyons, and the tee offers a breathtaking panorama that stretches for miles south across the Sonoran Desert into Mexico. Fazio said this hole was the "shortest and most expensive par 3 that I've ever designed." This one-shotter is a pure example of Fazio's design philosophy: "To visually intimidate the golfer, yet to have it play easier

than it looks." The Canyon course winds through the inspiring beauty of Esperrero Canyon and incorporates the massive rock formation known as Whaleback Rock.

Golf in an environmentally sensitive area is controversial, but careful development has ensured this resort's environmental integrity and provided exquisite scenery. Recognized for its conservation and preservation efforts, The Lodge at Ventana Canyon is a certified member of the Audubon Cooperative Sanctuary Program for Golf Courses, an internationally acclaimed program which promotes ecologically sound development and operation of golf facilities.

Although both courses are great examples of desert golf, most players give the edge to the Mountain course.

The first hole, a 422-yard par 4, allows for a fair introduction to the round, although the tee shot should favor the left side in order to have the best angle into the green. The

drive on the short, uphill second hole must be well struck in order to carry a ridge stretching across the fairway about 215 yards out. The best advice on the aforementioned par-3 third hole is, "Don't miss the green!" Desert, scrub, cactus, and other related nasties await the errant ball. Unfortunately for the first-timer, club selection is vital. One clue: This hole plays even shorter than the card indicates.

The par-5 fourth hole

VENTANA CANYON GOLF AND RACQUET CLUB
TUCSON, ARIZONA
CANYON COURSE

HOLE	YARDAGE	PAR			
1	408	4	10	336	4
2	483	5	11	463	4
3	401	4	12	574	5
4	290	4	13	158	3
5	148	3	14	303	4
6	464	4	15	474	4
7	552	5	16	221	3
8	183	3	17	442	4
9	416	4	18	503	5
OUT	3,345	36	IN	3,474	36
			TOTAL	6,819	72

favors the left-to-right player since a long bunker fills in the corner of the dogleg. A "church-pew" style series of bunkers lays in wait on the right side but should be out of play for all but the real slicer. The second shot should take into account the lake which runs alongside the fairway right up to the green. The fifth hole doglegs slightly left after a tee shot over water. Pot bunkers dot the right rough and punctuate the area surrounding the green. Left is death on the par-3 sixth where the perverse green slopes away from the incoming shot.

The Arizona desert provides spectacular settings, such as at the 12th green on the Canyon course.

On the seventh, the No. 1 stroke hole, a well-placed fairway bunker about 230 yards out catches more than its share of decent tee shots, and the very firm green is not receptive to the required mid- or long-iron approach on this longish par 4. Although the eighth hole is a par 5, it is not very long and may offer a birdie chance for the player who powers a drive down the middle. A super second shot will carry the 40-yard-wide waste area which rips across the fairway. Accuracy is more important than length on No. 9, a mid-length par 4. The green sits slightly below the fairway's plateau and is guarded closely behind by desert. Once again, club selection is critical to stay on the turf.

The back nine starts with a short par 4 where the right side of the fairway provides the best angle to a shallow green which slopes away from the player. A fairway wood or long-iron might be the best choice off the tee. Depending on the wind, a good drive on No. 11 could leave anything from a short-iron right up to a fairway wood, usually from a hilly lie. The 12th, a long par 5, requires three solid shots to this deep green. Hit it close or face a 60 or 70 foot putt. A fairway wood or long-iron off the 13th tee should leave an approach of 100 yards or less to a three-tiered green. Hit a mid-iron on the next tee to this side-hill par 3. Shots to the left may kick down onto the green, but don't count on it. Number 15 is a strong par 4 where a solid drive leaves an uphill approach to an elevated green protected by a large mound front left and the Whaleback Rock behind.

The 16th hole features a downhill tee shot to a very large green. Once again, club selection is vital; the hole plays shorter than its yardage, and you must be close to the hole to make birdie, or even par. A split fairway is the 17th's unique design feature, and the left side offers a shorter approach to the two-tiered green. The challenge on the 18th tee is to keep your concentration. Three accurate shots are required to reach the deep green filled with subtle rolls. The greenside bunker to the right stretches nearly 100 yards back into the fairway.

Although golf is a featured activity, The Lodge at Ventana Canyon has the beauty and amenities to stand on its own. The abundance of indigenous flora and fauna and its location in the Santa Catalina Mountains makes this luxurious resort a peaceful respite for nature lovers. Bordered by the Coronado National Forest and home to a 600-acre nature preserve, the resort is a haven for desert wildlife such as deer, rabbits, bobcats, coyotes, hawks, and quail. Vegetation also thrives at the resort as natural springs keep the property green and lush year-round. Tennis is another focus at The Lodge, and the adventurous can partake of other activities such as hot-air ballooning, desert jeep tours, horseback riding, soaring, rock climbing, mountain biking, and sky diving.

There is no second chance at the Mountain Course's tiny but terrifying third hole.

Stretching almost 600 yards through desert, cactus, and brush, the par-5 fourth hole on the Mountain course tests both length and accuracy.

A Breed Apart

Ventana Canyon is a creation of Tom Fazio, widely regarded as the finest active course architect. Starting out in the business as a teenager in 1962, he first worked with his uncle George until the late 1970s. The Wild Dunes layout in South Carolina brought him national attention, and he polished that reputation with designs of increasing imagination and style. Noteworthy examples include the Vintage Club in California, North Carolina's Wade Hampton, the Black Diamond Ranch in Florida, and the incredibly expensive Shadow Creek, built for casino owner Steve Wynn in Las Vegas.

North Carolina's Wade Hampton is spectacular, private, and one of the most rewarding courses to play in the world. Here is the par-4 eighth.

————— Cashiers, North Carolina —————

WADE HAMPTON

Golf Club

Architect: Tom Fazio
Opened for Play: 1987

High in the Blue Ridge Mountains of North Carolina, the village of Cashiers makes a bucolic setting for the secluded Wade Hampton Golf Club. Encircled by 28,000 acres of national forest and rising 3,500 feet above sea level, this area has retained the same natural beauty described by Thomas Wolfe in *Look Homeward Angel.*

Cashiers (pronounced "cash-ers") has been a favorite vacation spot for generations. Southern families are attracted by the cool summers and dramatic views of the mountains. In the early days, fishing was said to be the main attraction; golf was just one of several sporting activities along with boating, riding, and tennis. Later the popularity of golf grew, and many courses were built near Cashiers in the 1950s and 1960s. As a result, the area became widely known for the quality of its resort and retirement golf.

With the increasing number of golfers attracted to Cashiers, the need arose for something different — a true golf club,

TEES	LENGTH	PAR	RATING
FAZIO	7,154	72	74.4
MCKEE	6,839	72	72.0
WADE HAMPTON	6,431	72	70.9
FOUNDERS	5,934	72	68.5

WADE HAMPTON GOLF CLUB
CASHIERS, NORTH CAROLINA

HOLE	YARDAGE	PAR		HOLE	YARDAGE	PAR
1	544	5		10	564	5
2	456	4		11	172	3
3	219	3		12	317	4
4	581	5		13	416	4
5	419	4		14	410	4
6	158	3		15	429	4
7	386	4		16	489	4
8	401	4		17	196	3
9	442	4		18	555	5
OUT	3,606	36		IN	3,548	36
				TOTAL	7,154	72

one devoted exclusively to the game with a course designed for the dedicated golfer and maintained to a high standard. Thus, the Wade Hampton Golf Club was born.

The Wade Hampton golf course, opened in 1987, came near the end of a decade of remarkable new courses. This period might be characterized as the decade of spectacular designs, in which many innovative and exciting courses incorporated dramatic features. Wade Hampton is considered to be an example of design elements that have dominated golf course architecture throughout the years — both strategic and penal, difficult and friendly, a balance of new ideas and old traditions. The course is probably most memorable for its variety and subtlety of design, combined with breathtaking mountain views, set among stands of giant hardwoods and pines.

The Wade Hampton course is really four

courses in one, differentiated by their length: the Fazio (named after the architect, 7,154 yards), the McKee (named after the developer, 6,839 yards), the Wade Hampton (6,431 yards), and the Founders (5,934 yards). At any length, the course is very walkable and caddies are available.

Tom Fazio was selected as the designer of Wade Hampton because of his ability to create exciting golf while enhancing the natural beauty of the course setting. Fazio created a course that reflects both the spirit and the contours of the Blue Ridge Mountains. Natural rock outcroppings are brought into play, tee boxes are constructed of native stone, and mounds and bunkers complement the surrounding mountains.

Following its 1987 selection by *Golf Digest* as Best New Private Course in America, Wade Hampton rose quickly to national prominence, entering the magazine's Top 20 in 17th position two years later.

The par-3 17th hole epitomizes the Wade Hampton experience: an immaculate undulating fairway framed by a towering forest with Chimney Top Mountain presiding over the vista.

The par-3 sixth hole plays from an elevated tee to a well-guarded sloping green.

It continues to maintain a strong position in all such published rankings and is the top-ranked mountain course in the world on *Golf* magazine's Top 100 list.

The residential community at Wade Hampton is limited to 300 homes. A carefully structured development plan assures that the integrity of golf is not compromised by residential development; accordingly, homes with golf course frontage are confined to the perimeter of the course. No hole has homes on both sides of it, and many holes have no development at all. Since the course lies on the valley floor of a mountain bowl, some of the most dramatic homes are back away from the course on the surrounding ridges, with views of both the course and the mountains beyond.

The club is structured as a private, member-owned club with 300 golf members and no social members. Wade Hampton differs from most other clubs because it is strictly a golf club — there are no facilities for swimming, tennis, or other sports, and none are planned. There are, however, close relationships with several tennis and family clubs in the area which offer opportunities for membership. As is the case at many true golf clubs, the clubhouse at Wade Hampton is unpretentious and understated. It serves as a rendezvous for post-golf activity and offers quality dining with mountain hospitality.

The Origins Of Wade Hampton

The setting for Wade Hampton has an interesting history. The Cherokee Indians spent time here, using the area for a summer hunting ground. Throughout the years, arrowheads and other Indian artifacts have been found. For more than 150 years, the land was owned by the Hamptons of South Carolina. Wade Hampton III, the most famous family member and the one for whom the club was named, played a significant role in 19th-century Southern history. Known as "the giant in gray" of the Confederate Army, Hampton also served as governor of South Carolina and as a U.S. senator. Hampton spent his summers here as a young boy and returned to this mountain retreat throughout his long and colorful life. In 1922, the Hampton estate was purchased by industrialist E. Lyndon McKee, who converted it into a summer resort: High

Hampton Inn. An agreement in 1984 among his heirs allowed his grandchildren to acquire the undeveloped portion of the property to build the Wade Hampton Golf Club.

The 401-yard eighth hole requires a long, accurate drive to allow for an approach shot clear of the dogleg.

*The par-3 12th hole on Wild Dunes' Links
course shows why designer Tom Fazio
called this property "an architect's dream."*

—— *Charleston, South Carolina* ——

WILD DUNES

*Architect: Tom Fazio
Opened for Play: 1980*

The Links course at Wild Dunes has been called "a combination of Scotland and the Caribbean." Certainly, there can be little doubt that the finishing holes, flowing among dunes, inspire memories of the original links on the Atlantic's other shore, thousands of miles away.

Tom Fazio, or so the story goes, was offered a bet by the developer of Wild Dunes that he would agree that the piece of land was the best property for a golf course he had ever seen. Fazio examined the land and said, "I owe you $1,000."

"I saw right away that it was an architect's dream," Fazio recalled in an interview with *Golf Digest*. "It had all the elements you could ask for — trees, water, dunes, and an ocean coast. The routing was relatively easy because some of the holes looked like they had been

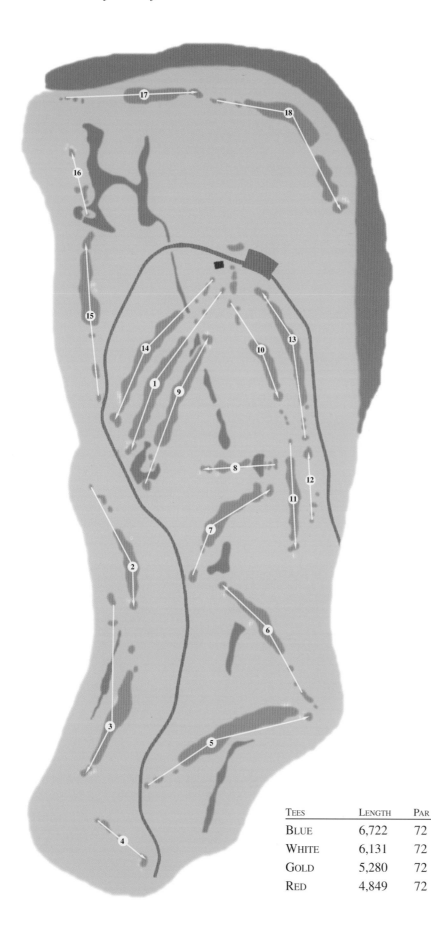

there forever. The place reminded me of Pine Valley...An architect comes across that kind of land only once or twice in a lifetime." It has been said that the Links course established Fazio's reputation as a first-class designer.

Despite the ravages of tropical storms and hurricanes — Hurricane Hugo forced a nine-month closing of the resort in 1989 — and the encroachment of condos, Wild Dunes remains a memorable destination. In addition to the Links course, the Harbor course offers a different level of challenge. Its six par 3s and shorter overall length offer more opportunities for higher handicappers to walk off the 18th green with a score they can be proud of. Of the Harbor course, opened in 1986 and renovated to par 70 in 1990, Fazio says "that, with maturity [it] would be thought of as being just as good, if not better, than the

WILD DUNES
CHARLESTON, SOUTH CAROLINA
LINKS COURSE

HOLE	YARDAGE	PAR
1	501	5
2	370	4
3	420	4
4	170	3
5	505	5
6	421	4
7	359	4
8	203	3
9	451	4
OUT	3,400	36
10	331	4
11	376	4
12	192	3
13	427	4
14	489	5
15	426	4
16	175	3
17	405	4
18	501	5
IN	3,322	36
TOTAL	6,722	72

TEES	LENGTH	PAR	RATING
BLUE	6,722	72	72.7
WHITE	6,131	72	69.7
GOLD	5,280	72	71.2
RED	4,849	72	69.1

Links." As well, Wild Dunes Tennis Center has been ranked sixth in the nation. Twenty swimming pools, miles of biking, hiking, and jogging trails, and top-notch convention facilities round out the package.

The course offers a "walking tour" description of the Links, not intended as a "how-to-play guide." The first hole is a straightforward 501-yard par 5 from the back tees with a generous fairway devoid of bunkers. The 370-yard second hole features salt marsh down its entire right side and can be deceptively difficult: "Just ask the guy who lost the 1985 U.S. Senior Amateur here — the 20th hole of the championship match —

to a par." A lengthy forced carry over salt marsh is the first indication that the third hole is anything but a pushover; more marsh guards the left-hand side of the green.

At 505 yards from the championship tees, the par-5 fifth hole seems reachable in two, on paper. But beware: The green is hidden just behind a pair of bookend dunes, each sporting a deep bunker gashed into its inner flank. On No. 6, stand on the scenic, elevated back tee and have faith that there is more fairway out there than you see. A big drive on this 421-yard par 4 gets you to the top of the hill on this rolling fairway, making your approach much easier. At 203 yards, the

Hard by the Atlantic, the par-4 17th hole on the Links course is a visual and golfing delight.

That Sinking Feeling

The 18th hole at the Links course is much more than a stunning and challenging golf hole: It also holds a significant spot in U.S. history. During the Revolutionary War, Lord Cornwallis's command of 2,000 soldiers landed there, planning to cross Breach Inlet to Sullivan's Island to attack Fort Moultrie from the rear. The English were met and held at bay by a force composed of 600 North and South Carolina regulars, a company of militia, and a company of Catawba Indians. Not a single soldier crossed over to Sullivan's Island that day. It was America's first major victory in the South. A century later, during the Civil War, the Confederate submarine *H. L. Hunley* rammed the Union warship USS *Housatonic* off the Isle of Palms. Although both ships eventually sank as a result of the collision, the episode is regarded as the world's first successful submarine attack in battle. Today, the *Housatonic*'s anchor rests just outside the Wild Dunes reception center.

Hitting the eighth green isn't easy, but it's child's play compared with one-putting this severely contoured green.

eighth is the longest par 3 on the course, and Fazio, in a benevolent mood, saw fit to design a large green. The bad news is that this putting surface is dramatically contoured and writing a "3" on your scorecard as you walk to the next tee should be viewed as a victory.

Number nine runs parallel to the first hole and, at 451 yards, is a long par 4. Hope the wind is at your back and bust it! The 10th is technically a drivable par 4, but the green is perched precariously atop a natural dune ridge. Even without the ocean's surf lapping at its borders, the par-3 12th has to be one of the most photogenic holes in golf. The green is tucked into the dunes, a manicured oasis

amidst a hostile desert. The 13th concludes what Fazio calls the "dunes holes." Set in the dunesland that cradles the previous three holes, this 427-yard par 4 features a green surrounded by native landforms. One visit to the dunes and you will have fond thoughts of ordinary, man-made bunkers.

The final three holes are breathtakingly pretty. Sixteen is a 175-yard par 3 with a postage-stamp green encircled by marsh and water. Numbers 17 and 18, stretching along the Atlantic, have been so frequently photographed and featured in the resort's advertising that many golfers feel they have already played them.

The 17th (shown) and 18th holes at the Links course leave the player exhilarated and eager to return.

———— Mamaroneck, New York ————

WINGED FOOT

Golf Club

Architect: A. W. Tillinghast
Opened for Play: 1923

The title of Winged Foot Golf Club's history by Douglas Smith contains the words "the friendly trees." Although Winged Foot is known for its variety and number of trees, Smith's book says almost 8,000 trees were cut down to facilitate A. W. Tillinghast's 36-hole layout over 280 acres. "Tillie the Terror" was indeed living up to his nickname on this project, which would be one of his last and, many attest, his best. For in addition to solving any potential firewood shortage in the immediate vicinity for several years, the project also required 24,000 cubic yards of earth for greens; 7,200 tons of rock blasted to allow for fairways and bunkers; 21,000 feet of drain pipe; 25,000 feet of irrigation pipe; and 14 tons of grass seed — all of this through the efforts of 220 men, 60 teams of horses, and 19 tractors.

WINGED FOOT GOLF CLUB
MAMARONECK, NEW YORK
WEST COURSE

HOLE	YARDAGE	PAR			
1	446	4	10	190	3
2	411	4	11	386	4
3	216	3	12	535	5
4	453	4	13	212	3
5	515	5	14	418	4
6	324	4	15	417	4
7	166	3	16	457	5
8	442	4	17	449	4
9	471	5	18	448	4
OUT	3,444	36	IN	3,512	36
			TOTAL	6,956	72

TEES	LENGTH	PAR	RATING
CHAMPIONSHIP	6,956	72	73.2
REGULAR	6,560	72	73.2

"Give us a man-sized course," the founders told Tillinghast. And history attests that he did that and more. "As the various holes came to life, they were of a sturdy breed," Tillinghast wrote of Winged Foot. "The contouring of the greens places a premium on the placement of the drives, but never is there the necessity of facing a prodigious carry of the sink-or-swim sort. It is only the knowledge that the next shot must be played with rifle accuracy that brings the realization that the drive must be placed. The holes are like men, all rather similar from foot to neck, but with the greens showing the same varying characters as human faces." Thus did Winged Foot become, in many minds, a showcase of the "strategic" school of course architecture, although no less an authority than Robert Trent Jones cites Tillinghast's bunkering at Winged Foot as exemplary of "heroic" design. One thing is sure: The design is the ultimate "tough but fair" test and definitely not of the "penal" approach to architecture which has a devout, and possibly demented, following.

Hale Irwin, who won the 1974 U.S. Open here, is a discerning student of all aspects of golf, including architecture. In Winged Foot's club history, he is quoted as telling the author, "On

Tillinghast courses, the thing that comes to mind are the subtleties of his holes. He worked his holes to the land. Today's architects work the land to the holes because of the equipment they have. Tillinghast and those early architects didn't have such equipment, and they used the terrain as it was...But as to Winged Foot, I like it also for the strategic course it is. I prefer the architect who employs the 'stratagem of placement.' It's the best test of golf."

While both the East and the West courses were laid out by Tillinghast and both opened the same year and both have legions of fans among their members, it is the West course that has become more prominent

among golf fans in general for its tournament preeminence. Some argue that the greatest moment in the championship history of Winged Foot West came in the very first U.S. Open it ever hosted.

On June 29, 1929, Robert Tyre Jones Jr. had a comfortable six-shot lead over Al Espinosa. Espinosa, trailing the great "Bobby" Jones by such a margin, could very well have simply cruised in for second place. But as Espinosa relaxed, his game reached a crescendo: He played the last six holes in 22 strokes for a four-round total of 294. Meanwhile, Jones was crashing: bogeying the 13th, taking seven at the 15th, and three-putting 16 from

The par-5 ninth on the West course plays as a par 4 in championships.

The 13th hole on the East course is renowned as one of the most beautiful spots at Winged Foot.

20 feet. Suddenly, he needed to finish 4-4 in order to tie Espinosa and force the playoff. Jones made four at 17 and smacked a good drive down the middle on 18. His approach shot was short, catching a poor lie in heavy rough just short of a bunker. His desperate wedge out stopped 12 feet from the hole. He made the putt, just barely, and dominated Espinosa in the 36-hole playoff the following day. Sportswriter Grantland Rice was in attendance and put the situation in perspective: "If Bobby had missed that great putt...I

do not believe he would have gone on to achieve his great victory a year later when he won the Grand Slam of Golf [the British Open and Amateur and the U.S. Open and Amateur]... I will always believe that the remainder of Jones's career hung on that putt."

In addition to the 1929 thriller, Winged Foot has played host to three other U.S. Opens. In 1959, Billy Casper used his fine bunker play to claim the title. Looking back at the 1974 version, won by Hale Irwin with a four-round total of seven over par, Arnold

One Of The Best

The 10th hole on Winged Foot's West course is acknowledged as an exceptional par 3. Ben Hogan likened the tee shot to "hitting a 3-iron into someone's bedroom." Architect A. W. Tillinghast called it the best par 3 he ever designed. At 183 yards from the back tees, its length is not the challenge. Rather, it is the subtle, elevated, and well-bunkered green target that frustrates most players.

Palmer reminisced about the course where he almost collected another Open title: "I feel that Winged Foot is one of the finest of the traditional golf courses in the world. As an architect, course designer and builder, as well as a player, I have enjoyed it from every aspect." As the 1984 Open (won by Fuzzy Zoeller) approached, Ben Hogan, an honorary Winged Foot member, recollected: "It is an old course, one of those that can stand up to any of the newer ones for the quality of shots required. I had heard it described as a course on which you can use every club in your bag, one of the best tests there is, and I found this to be true, because I have used them all there." U.S. Women's Opens were played here in 1957 (won by Jackie Pung) and 1972 (won by Susie Maxwell Berning). The inaugural U.S. Senior Open was won here by Roberto DeVicenzo in 1980.

Joe Dey, a highly respected golf administrator who held the top post at both the United States Golf Association and the Professional Golfers' Association of America, summed up the Winged Foot experience: "The very name Winged Foot has a sort of magic for those who know the club from afar. To them it stands for competitive golf at its highest level — a place where history was made by Bobby Jones, Tommy Armour, Richard D. Chapman, Billy Casper, Hale Irwin, Jacqueline Pung, Susie Maxwell Berning, Roberto DeVicenzo, and others. For those who know Winged Foot intimately, it is much more fun and meaningful than a place of big occasions. It is a steady heartbeat of golfing pleasure and sportsmanship, where the game is the thing and where many great matches and tall tales have been spun. Winged Foot is, in sum, a temple of the spirit of golf."

PHOTOGRAPHIC CREDITS

Unless otherwise noted, all photographs in this book are by Michael French. Doug Ball, 110 (top); Champions Golf Club, 38 (top); Robert Trent Jones Florida Inc., 206 (top); Plainfield Country Club, 158 (bottom); Dennis Roberson, Colonial Country Club, (46-51); Royal Canadian Golf Association, 79, 103, 189 (top), 200 (top); Phil Sheldon, Augusta National Golf Club, 10-15; Cypress Point Golf Club, 52-57; Pine Valley Golf Club, 148-153; Tennessee PGA Junior Golf Academy, 75 (top); Don Vickery, 45 (bottom), 68 (top).

BIBLIOGRAPHY

We are grateful for permission being granted to reprint materials from the following books.
Baltusrol, 100 Years. Progress Printing, 1995.
Cornish, Geoffrey, and Ronald Whitten. *The Architects of Golf.* HarperCollins, 1993.
Cornish, Geoffrey, and Ronald Whitten. *The Golf Course.* The Rutledge Press, 1988.
Hornung, Paul. *Scioto Country Club, 75 Years of History.* Scioto Country Club, 1993.
Kladstrup, Donald. *The Crown Jewels of Oak Hill.* Oak Hill Country Club, 1989.
Kladstrup, Donald. *Evolution of a Legacy.* Oak Hill Country Club, 1995.
Prairie Dunes, The First Fifty Years. Mennonite Press, 1987.
Shackelford, Geoff. *The Riviera Country Club, A Definitive History.* The Riviera Country Club, 1995.
Tollhurst, Desmond. *Golf At Merion.* Merion Golf Club, 1989.

The author acknowledges the following publications as being useful in the research for this book. Where extended excerpts were used, every effort was made to secure permission for reprint.
Doak, Tom. *The Confidential Guide to Golf Courses.* Sleeping Bear Press, 1996.
Jones, Robert Trent. *Golf By Design.* Little Brown and Company, 1993.
Palmer, Arnold, with Barry Furlong. *Go For Broke!* Bantam Books, 1973.
Peper, George. *Golf Courses of the PGA Tour.* Times Mirror Books, 1986.